DEDICATION

❧

*I'd like to dedicate this book
to the body of believers
here at Calvary Worship Center,
and to my lovely wife, Norma,
who has stood by me
in every spiritual battle
down through the years.*

*Thank you, honey,
for your prayers,
love, and support;
for being there,
in the good and bad times.*

CONTENTS

❦

FOREWORD

⁓⋊⁓

Satan would have us believe that we are helpless against his devices, but the opposite is true. To believe this lie is to believe God has ill prepared His people for the times in which we live. God is a loving Father, who not only provides us with the grace and mercy we need, but also the power and weaponry of spiritual warfare, that we might live as overcomers, rather than underachievers.

In order to live according to His strength and not our weakness, it is essential, in today's spiritual climate, to be equipped with that which our Father has given us. Satan wants us to lose sight of the fact that the warfare we are engaged in is spiritual and therefore must be waged in the Spirit. This book reminds us that the forces of darkness are far more frightened of the weakest believer than that believer should ever be of them.

It was the great English poet and hymnodist William Cowper who said *"Satan trembles when he sees the weakest Christian on his knees."* I pray God will be glorified through your life as you seek to employ, by faith, the principles of His undeniable and indisputable truth!

1

The Great Battle

We are locked in a battle. This is not a friendly, gentleman's discussion. It is a life and death conflict between the spiritual hosts of wickedness and those who claim the name of Christ.
—Francis A. Schaeffer

A War for Everyone

During World War II, it is estimated that twenty million soldiers lost their lives. But that doesn't tell the whole story of global devastation, because over fifty million citizens and non-combatants were also killed. So we see that many people who were not even fighting on the battlefield were victims of warfare. War was a fact of life, whether the world wanted it or not.

Christians must come to understand that earth is a battleground and not a playground. Just as nearly the whole population on earth was jeopardized by the events of World War II, everyone who has ever been alive is made subject to a severe spiritual war that is taking place on this planet during their time on earth.

There is a word for those who think they can remain neutral in this spiritual battle—victims! Sometimes the gospel is misrepresented as an immediate doorway to a life free of problems, but experience and biblical common sense show that this is not so.

First of all, anyone who does not have a relationship with Jesus Christ cannot even be aware of the jeopardy they are in. This is because an unconverted person cannot perceive spiritual reality. Moreover, they have limited ability to receive truth; it's like a radio without an antenna—no reception is possible. This is why non-Christians can read the Bible and see none of the revelation that believers find. Until the Spirit of God is "installed," there's no reception!

Blind Hostages

So, this group is like blind captives in the spiritual war raging around them. They march to the orders of their fallen nature, are given over to lust and are willingly subject to all manner of spiritual strangeness. Unless they repent and their eyes are opened, they will remain hostages to their dying breath and beyond.

> *But the natural man does not receive the things of the Spirit of God, for they are foolishness to him; nor can he know them, because they are spiritually discerned.* 1 Corinthians 2:14

There is a spiritual realm that is actually the ultimate reality, invisible, but not inferior to the physical world. In fact, the visible is a result of what is manifesting from the spiritual. The natural man without Christ is subject to forces he cannot comprehend, much less master. It

is only the born-again, spirit-filled believer who can begin to grasp the scale of the supernatural conflict surrounding us.

The Deep Back Story

The leader of the opposition to all those who have called upon Christ is the Devil. The word *Satan*, the name given to our adversary, means *accuser, one who brings a charge*. Before Christians march off into battle, it is wise to be informed about the Enemy, his history, values, and goals.

There have been many famous traitors throughout history. Some do it for love, some for money, others for pride or revenge. Benedict Arnold betrayed the cause of the American Revolution, Brutus raised a dagger to Julius Caesar, and the infamous kiss of Judas Iscariot led Roman soldiers to the Son of God.

These acts of high treason are all over-shadowed by the ultimate betrayal, when Lucifer, Son of the Morning, led a rebellion in heaven.

Since we view this scene through dim light, the magnitude of this betrayal is almost impossible to grasp. It is hard to picture exactly what took place, but Ezekiel chapter twenty-eight records the amazing story of spiritual wickedness in heavenly places. We can be assured that since God is aware of everything in every place, the planning and execution of this rebellion did not come as an ambush.

You were in Eden, the garden of God; Every precious stone was your covering:The sardius,

3

*topaz, and diamond, Beryl, onyx, and jasper,
Sapphire, turquoise, and emerald with gold.
The workmanship of your timbrels and pipes
was prepared for you on the day you were
created.* Ezekiel 28:13

Imagine! Before his fall, Lucifer was highly exalted in the ranks of angels. It appears he enjoyed unique privileges that have now been revoked, or at least restricted. As we read these verses, we are glimpsing ancient events of a high and holy history that is almost too amazing for our human minds to entertain.

*"You were the anointed cherub who covers; I
established you; you were on the holy mountain
of God; you walked back and forth in the midst
of fiery stones.* Ezekiel 28:14

This is another intriguing look behind the celestial curtain, as God chastises a favored angel. What it means for Lucifer to have this heavenly hall pass is not clear, but it must have meant something special! Lucifer is one of very few angels whose names are revealed in scripture; Michael and Gabriel are the others. This fact alone reveals that he enjoyed a special place.

The Original Domino

There is no way to know how long this condition continued, yet at some point, it went wrong, terribly wrong. We can tell from scripture that angels have a different level of relationship with God than man does. For now, at least, they truly are heaven's super heroes. It would not be surprising if many of the myths and legends that developed in Greece, Rome, and Egypt were rooted in some facet of the angel-demonic conflict. In any case, Lucifer ended badly.

> *You were perfect in your ways from the day you were created, Till iniquity was found in you.* Ezekiel 28:15

Philosophers and poets have long pondered the original cause for the negative effects we find in the human condition. We need look no further than this critical juncture where evil is first found. We can observe from the sequence of the creation story in Genesis that all things were good until this point.

> *Then God saw everything that He had made, and indeed it was very good. So the evening and the morning were the sixth day.* Genesis 1:31

The birth of wickedness is found here, and nothing would ever be the same.

> *"By the abundance of your trading You became filled with violence within, and you sinned; Therefore I cast you as a profane thing out of the mountain of God; and I destroyed you, O covering cherub, from the midst of the fiery stones."* Ezekiel 28:16

Lucifer, filled with pride and envy, was now cast out of his first estate, and he had nowhere to go but down. Somewhere in this sequence of events, his nature warped and his name changed from Lucifer, *bearer of light,* to Satan, *the accuser*. This incredible transaction had repercussions that reverberated through the universe to the present.

> *For we know that the whole creation groans and labors with birth pangs together until now.* Romans 8:22

True to his name, according to Revelation 12:7-11, Satan goes before the throne of God, accusing us day and night. Perhaps you have never been in court hearing charges read against you, but courtroom dramas have made this a familiar scene. The human race stands guilty of the sins Satan charges it with. Thanks to God that He provided a solution to our guilt!

> *Then I heard a loud voice saying in heaven, 'Now salvation, and strength, and the kingdom of our God, and the power of His Christ have come, for the accuser of our brethren, who accused them before our God day and night, has been cast down.* Revelation 12:10

This is when we see Satan for the pretender he truly is! We have all watched, in recent years, when tyrants such as Saddam Hussein and Moammar Kadafi were tracked down and removed from power. Both had enjoyed long, evil reigns where they caused great harm from their temporary thrones of power. Yet, at the end of their day, both these rulers were displayed for what they really were—merely men who arrogantly abused their authority.

What a Day!

We find more dramatic insight from Isaiah, where the Bible tells us Satan was cast down by God from Heaven because of his pride and arrogance. His vain imagination led him to believe he would sit on the very throne of God!

> *"How you are fallen from heaven, O Lucifer, son of the morning! How you are cut down to the ground, You who weakened the nations!* Isaiah 14:12

Why God allowed Satan to recruit angels into his demonic realm is a question that will have to wait. What we do know is that the Devil's downfall was rooted in pride.

> *For you have said in your heart: 'I will ascend into heaven, I will exalt my throne above the stars of God; I will also sit on the mount of the congregation on the farthest sides of the north;'* Isaiah 14:13

Amazingly, the Devil did not go alone, Revelation indicates that Satan took one-third of the angels with him when he rebelled. This had to be the greatest sales job in history. How did so many angels join the legions of Lucifer/Satan? It seems unimaginable that so many super-intelligent beings could be led to rebel against God Himself.

> *His tail drew a third of the stars of heaven and threw them to the earth...* Revelation 12:4 (a)

It did happen, and the book of Jude tells of angels who sinned and were judged; these angels have no hope of redemption.

Get A Grip

We must get a grip on the total battlefield scenario. First of all, Satan is doomed. He has no hope of victory or restoration. And yet, he remains a force to be reckoned with. For His own purposes, God has arranged for this conflict to afflict His church—for now. We must become comfortable with the principle that heaven retains the right to mysteries that we cannot understand. It is clear that something much larger than ourselves is taking place in the universe; the interaction between God and Satan has dimensions beyond our finding out. However, a great deal has been revealed to us. Therefore, we must become fully informed and actively involved in our position in the battle.

> *"But you are cast out of your grave like an abominable branch, [like] the garment of those who are slain, thrust through with a sword, who go down to the stones of the pit, like a corpse trodden underfoot."* Isaiah 14:19

It is important that we take time to get this background, because someday soon Satan will be totally humbled; his pride will finally lead to his downfall. When that day comes, believers will look upon him and marvel that this creature caused so much havoc for so long.

War On

The war is on; that is not in question. Satan has no way to ever touch or attack the Lord Himself, so he vents his fury on the object of God's love—His church. And while it may not seem comfortable to be in the cross-hairs of an invisible, super-powerful enemy who would like to destroy us, the church has more than hope—we have absolute certain victory! This confidence is not the result of our mad spiritual skills, but because of who our general is!

> *But we speak the wisdom of God in a mystery, the hidden wisdom which God ordained before the ages for our glory, which none of the rulers of this age knew; for had they known, they would not have crucified the Lord of glory.*
> 1 Corinthians 2:7-8

So, we see that God's plan overwhelmed and outflanked what Satan engineered. He hoped the death of Jesus would be his path to power, but it became his road to ruin. Satan's destiny is sealed, but what is not clear is how believers will perform in the few years they have been given on earth. The issue becomes whether we will take advantage of the victory that is available to us or forfeit the fantastic privileges and opportunities we have been granted.

Facing Reality

When the sailors and soldiers at Pearl Harbor woke up on December 7, 1941, they found a peaceful Hawaiian morning that would not last long. Soon, Japanese planes would rain death and havoc on the Pacific Fleet at anchor in Oahu. The next day, President Franklin Roosevelt went before a joint session of Congress and announced that a "state of war" existed between the United States and Japan. This declaration made official what already existed and allowed resources to be immediately channeled into the war effort.

When a person accepts the offer of Jesus Christ for forgiveness and salvation, he or she is entering into spiritual warfare with the forces of evil. Before that time, they were blindly cooperating with satanic forces in their destructive campaign against God and heaven.

For children of light, spiritual war is a daily reality. What many Christians need to do is come to a personal realization of this fact and actively enter into combat in order to enjoy the victory that has been provided for us.

2

Satanic Strategies
AND TACTICS

*The Devil is a better theologian than any of us
and is a devil still.*　　　　　—A.W. Tozer

Before you can actually be successful in spiritual battle, you need to clearly understand two military terms: *strategy* and *tactics*. *Strategy* refers to a plan of action designed to achieve an overall goal, where *tactics* are concerned with the conduct of individual conflicts or battles. Notice this: Satan constantly energizes tactics against the saints of God, even though he has a strategy that he knows will ultimately fail. Revelation tells us that Satan becomes enraged because he knows defeat is certain.

> *"Woe to the inhabitants of the earth and the sea!
> For the devil has come down to you, having great
> wrath, because he knows that he has a short time."*
> Revelation 12:12b

If Satan has a sane moment, he realizes his clock is running down, but far from surrendering to the inevitable, he rages on against the saints of God.

This explains a great mystery of the faith; although we are already declared victors and are more than conquerors, we must still go through the fog of spiritual war until the final day.

The grand strategies of Satan will not—cannot—prevail; his defeat is inevitable. In the meantime his tactics of warfare must be dealt with.

Thinking About the Unthinkable

Modern terrorism has introduced America to a form of warfare that is as repulsive as it can be effective. Unthinkable acts of homicide bombing on an individual and mass scale have become a pervasive and critical threat to our security. U.S. military deaths from acts of terrorism often exceed combat fatalities in the current theaters of war. Suicidal terrorism is not a new phenomenon. Long ago, Japanese culture developed kamikaze warfare that was unleashed against Allied Forces in World War II. Wave after wave of Japanese pilots were willing to purposefully crash their planes into their enemy. We can be sure that the same spirit that inspired kamikaze pilots is at work in those who germinate their modern plots of mass destruction. Since the bombing of the Beirut Marine barracks in 1983, there have been over 300 recorded cases of suicide bombings worldwide. This is a mind-boggling use of tactics. How do you defeat an enemy whose death is an instrument of attack? The answer speaks loudly into the lives of Christians who are subject to spiritual terrorism: Information comes first, we can not afford to be ignorant.

Information: Know Thy Enemy

Military intelligence is a crucial part of conducting a war. An accurate assessment of an enemy's assets and position is vital. A general must know the strength and location of enemy forces.

Jesus summarized the goals of Satan by saying that he has come to steal, rob, and destroy. It is pointless to try to understand this warped mind, so we must stay close to scripture for our information about his power and plans. So much of what Christians tend to believe about Satan is rooted in fiction, legend, and fantasy. Movies and myths have created a false and terrifying persona for this wicked, fallen angel. He is not to be minimized, but he is not to be feared. A well-informed, well-armed Christian soldier can advance daily into the battle, fully confident of success.

> *Lest Satan should get an advantage of us: for we are not ignorant of his devices.*
> 2 Corinthians 2:11

When Paul wrote this insightful letter, Corinth was a large city in Greece, overflowing with pagan idolatry. The Corinthian landscape was dotted with many temples to gods and goddesses. The city was filled with many different doctrines imported from foreign lands and distributed by the commercial trade that coursed through Corinth. When we consider Satan's ploys, it is easy to be diverted by the smokescreen of extreme cults, non-Christian religions, and pagan activity. Certainly the slick lies of Satan have begotten many false spiritual activities. Yet, Satan's main arena for action is not in false religions, but in the one true religion! Christianity stands as the only legitimate threat to Satan, and so this is where he works hardest to dim the light of truth.

Anything but the Main Thing

Satan understands the power of the cross of Jesus Christ; therefore he is devoted to keeping the church from proclaiming this liberating, life-changing truth. Forgiveness is our best friend and Satan's worst nightmare. When Christians dwell at the foot of the cross, they become marvelously unified on this level ground. Unity means massive power, so Satan will seek to divide the brethren, sow seeds of discord, and encourage slander and bitterness. When Christians fail to forgive each other, prayers are paralyzed, hearts are frozen, and hell rejoices. It is only logical that the reverse is also true. When we exhibit God's grace in large and small ways, His love and truth shine brightly, and darkness has no choice but to flee.

Consider this: while Satan's dramatic fireworks may get maximum attention, his real goal is to keep us from unleashing the power of the cross, because against its life-giving work he has no weapon. Satan and his minions are bold and shameless. Brazen lies, blasphemy, and bitter seduction of the saints are their stock-in-trade. However, the shadow of the cross is one place that fallen angels fear to tread.

Paul also warns us, however, that even though Satan is not all-knowing and omnipresent, he is a powerful, determined enemy. We see his plan in obvious operation through a wide variety of situations and circumstances, but the goal is always the same—divide the church, distract from the Great Commission, and dilute the pure gospel message.

A Scriptural Solution

The remedy for ignorance is knowledge and experience. This certainly does not mean we need to overemphasize the Devil. Our ignorance concerns the Word of God and what it says about who we are in Christ. God's word is light, and as it illuminates the deception of the enemy, we see clearly and the fog of deception is lifted. The Bible tells us that Satan is so deceptive that he's actually disguised himself as an angel of light. Remember, every light is not illumination; some of it can blind you into ignorance.

While there is some debate in the church about the reality of a literal, personal devil, Jesus and the Bible have no such controversy. Jesus spoke plainly of Satan numerous times, to all kinds of audiences. In John 8:44 he blasted the Pharisees with this gem: "You are of your father, the Devil." That did not improve his popularity around the temple.

Satan was, Jesus said, a murderer from the beginning, and does not stand in the truth because there is no truth in him, and he is the father of lies. Of course, Jesus had special insight into Satan because He had seen it all.

Jesus said:

And He said to them, "I saw Satan fall like lightning from heaven. Luke 10:18

15

3

Castles of the Soul

"Our past may explain why we're suffering but we must not use it as an excuse to stay in bondage."
　　　　　　　　　　　　　　　—JOYCE MEYER

For the weapons of our warfare are not carnal but mighty, to the pulling down of strongholds.
2 Corinthians 5:4 (a)

In medieval times, the castle was a strong fortification that was both a military stronghold and a social safe place. For centuries, castles were the focal point of invading armies and the defensive strategy for existing city-states.

When an enemy force invaded, the tactics often involved first establishing a foothold then attacking the fortified cities.

The forces of Satan use the same approach when it comes to conquering a soul or neutralizing a Christian.

First, Satan establishes a beachhead in your thought life, perhaps just an indulgent lustful fantasy or a preoccupation with a luxury. These invisible, seemingly harmless past distractions soon take on a life of their own. They can move swiftly from momentary reflections to increasingly strong thought patterns.

Learn a lesson from your computer. You have only so much bandwidth and storage space.

When illicit thoughts begin to clog our channels, something has to give. The carnal can dominate the spiritual because of the fundamental fallen state of the human condition. This is when the initial base camp of the enemy begins to spread and infiltrate with the ultimate goal of constructing a castle in your soul.

Whoever has no rule over his own spirit Is like a city broken down, without walls. Proverbs 25:28

An Unguarded City

It is possible for Christians to forfeit the full liberty and power that God freely offers to all who accept the forgiveness of His Son Jesus Christ.

Entire lives can be lived out in a forgiven state, yet shackled in the vise grip of bondage. A person can be saved, but stranded in unhealthy habits, patterns of destructive behavior and cycles of defeat.

Scripture clearly acknowledges this situation and warns against ignoring the progression of bondage. Satan's strategy for building strongholds is based on a familiar principle in his handbook of spiritual warfare: lying.

When Adam and Eve innocently faced the test in the Garden, Satan offered them something they already had.

"God knows you will be like Him if you partake of the fruit," the Serpent hissed. News flash! Adam and Eve were already made in the image of God. They sacrificed so much to receive a gift they possessed. So it is with so many spiritual strongholds.

"Take this, drink that, sleep with that person, and you will find peace and meaning in your life.

When Christians take this bait, they ignore the bold promises of the Bible that say Jesus is our peace, freedom and identity. Swallowing the lie of external fulfillment is crossing the threshold on a path to painful and powerful spiritual strongholds in your life.

The Power of Propaganda

Tell a lie often enough and strongly enough and soon, people will begin to believe it.

The Nazi's knew this. They convinced one of the most educated populations in history that the Jews and others were subhuman. Millions paid with their lives because of this wicked lie. Themedia understands this principle, so they assault society with slick campaigns designed to promote discontent that can supposedly be relieved by their products.

The road to destructive spiritual strongholds is paved with deception, defilement and depression.

When you are deceived into believing you need something more than God offers, the door to defilement is opened. Once you have tasted that fruit and found it addictive, a certain cycle begins.

19

Deception is based upon a lie; defilement is a function of failing to recognize that your body is a temple of the Holy Spirit. Depression soon follows, accompanied by self-condemnation. Completing the loop, you engage in more destructive behavior to self-medicate the depression, putting yourself into a spiritual death spiral.

The frequency of depression within the church is disturbing. How can God's people, who have been given so much and promised so much, lead lives that are entangled in bondage? The answer my friend is, spiritual strongholds.

What to do, what to do?

Arguing With A Liar

Yet Michael the archangel, in contending with the devil, when he disputed about the body of Moses, dared not bring him a reviling accusation, but said, "The Lord rebuke you!" Jude 1:9

It has become more than a passing fad for Christians to talk to Satan, rebuke him and command him. However, this tactic is not wise or productive. First, Satan is not impressed by you, then importantly, an archangel refused to rebuke the devil!

What if we could converse with Satan? Jesus said he was a liar from the start, so what is the purpose of a conversation? Better to follow the pattern of Jesus: Quote scripture and leave.

Another dead end in the effort to destroy spiritual strongholds is to trust in the power of what the Bible calls "will-worship." Once you acknowledge the presence of self-destructive behavior and habits, you have the right idea in destroying them, but then execute the attack with self power. You know what that feels like. "This is the last time, tomorrow I am going to stop." How is that working out for you?

Will-worship won't work.

Identity Theft

One in five Americans will at some point be affected by identity theft, our mobile, digital society is increasingly fertile ground for this crime. Losing your credit or credentials is painful but this is not the worst sort of identity theft. When man, made in the image of God, allows lies to obscure his position as the crown of creation, a high spiritual felony has taken place. This is the condition that allows the erection of counterfeit spiritual strongholds in your life. They are sold under the disguise of offering to upgrade you, but they are the worst kind of Trojan horse.

Satan must lie, because of his nature, and because of his product. If he came door-to door-and said, "Do this and it will eventually bring you into bondage and ruin your life." his closing sales numbers would be very low. So, he uses the propaganda techniques of glittering generalities and bandwagon pressure. "Great things will happen if you do this" and "Besides, everyone is doing it," have been the cornerstones of Satanic attack from day one.

The first correct step to the destruction of enemy fortified positions in your life is to fully understand your identity in Christ. Remember, you are not your habit; you must confess that you have behaved like an addict and repent by the power of the Holy Spirit, but you are a new creation in Christ.

Humble yourself, the Bible says, under God's mighty hand and He will lift you up.

Old Castles and Strong Towers

Until the advent of gunpowder and explosives in the Middle Age, castles were the most formidable structures in warfare. You can learn from one of the tactics used to attack castles: Surround them and starve them out. This approach means depriving your unhealthy habits of reinforcements. Struggling with lust? Lose the premium cable TV channels. Is substance abuse your dragon? Head for the health club instead of happy hour. This strategy will undermine the superstructure of an enemy stronghold and weaken it causing its walls to crumble.

When you boldly confess what the Bible says about you and your future, the blatant lies you formerly believed begin to pale and fade.

No one says it will be easy or quick, but the victory can be yours, and you have help.

What really brought the castle age to an end was the invention of explosives. Even the strongest castle could not stand against cannons and gunpowder charges beneath its walls.

The Holy Spirit is your dynamite! In Acts 1:8, Jesus promised His followers power when the Holy Spirit came upon them.

The word translated as power in our English Bible is the Greek word dynamis, the same root word that gives us dynamite.

The Holy Spirit literally offers you sticks of dynamite to blast away anything that is unlike the image of God in your lifestyle or character.

To experience the power of the Holy Spirit, you must acknowledge your total inability to conquer these Satanic strongholds using your own strength and acknowledge complete dependence on God. Remember, the weapons of your warfare are not carnal, but mighty to the pulling down of strongholds.

This is when the walls of deceit tumble. Here is where you find victory over a lifelong habit and this is the only way to recover your true identity in Christ.

When these enemy castles are destroyed, do not leave the land vacant! The Lord will supervise construction of strong towers of praise, prayer and the power found in being His child.

The name of the Lord is a strong tower, the righteous run into it, and they are saved. Proverbs 18:10

4

Invisible Darkness

Satan does not care how many people read about prayer if only he can keep them from praying.
—Paul E. Billheimer

Professional wrestling is fake. I hope this has not come as a shock to any of you. Every match is rigged, every outcome planned. That does not mean there is no real action in the ring. Olympic Slams, Camel Clutches, and Leaping Scissor Kicks require athletic skill and practice. Pro wrestlers can get injured even if the outcome of their match is set in stone. This illustrates what takes place in the match between Satan and man, without the soap opera drama themes and the capes. Yes, the struggle is authentic, but there is never a question as to which locker room will have the final victory celebration.

> *For we do not wrestle against flesh and blood, but against principalities, against powers, against the rulers of darkness of this age, against spiritual wickedness in heavenly places.*
> Ephesians 6:12

Science fiction is one of the most popular genres in movie making. In fact, several of the most popular films of all time are from this category. *Star Wars, E.T., Close Encounters of a Third Kind,* and other sci-fi titles have captured the American imagination and attention. Part of the attraction of science fiction comes from our interest in encountering the supernatural.

Who needs science fiction when we have biblical facts about how the unseen world functions? Darth Vader has nothing on the real Prince of Darkness! Although the struggles of Luke Skywalker against the dark side of the Force may have entertained us in two-hour installments, we are going in the ring every day and encountering the forces of a very real kingdom.

Paul tells the Ephesians that as Christians we are in a wrestling match—that we have to wrestle—against principalities and powers. Now notice, wrestling really denotes hand-to-hand combat. In other words, God has called you as a believer to fight. Paul said, "I fought the good fight of faith." So what about, "I just want to be a spectator; I do not want to get in the ring." Well then, you will be relegated to the category of being lukewarm, because you're sitting in a position where you're not exercising your faith, and if you don't exercise your faith, you will become disengaged. Faith without works is dead; God has called us to be followers of Jesus Christ. We need to be willing to fight. Anything worth having, you have to make a stand for. Daniel discovered this truth when an angel explained how warfare can delay answered prayer.

Daniel and the Devil

Satan cannot stop the work of God in your life, but he can restrain it. A prime example of this principle is found in the story of Daniel in the Old Testament. We know he was a man of prayer. Within his story a curtain is parted to give us a glimpse of some genuine spiritual combat associated with prayer. Prayer may seem calm and peaceful, but we find that behind the scenes, there is a battle raging.

> *Then he said to me, 'Do not fear, Daniel, for from the first day that you set your heart to understand, and to humble yourself before your God, your words are heard; and I have come because of your words.* Daniel 10:12

Briefly, the veil is lifted and in Daniel chapter ten we learn that as soon as Daniel began to pray, the answer was on the way, but Satan delayed its delivery for three weeks! In fact, this holding action required Michael, a heavyweight from heaven, to provide backup and get things moving. For three weeks Daniel prayed patiently, and it paid off. So saints, do not grow weary in the well-doing of prayer. Jesus counseled that men should always pray and not faint. I am sure Daniel was thankful he did not cease praying on day twenty!

So far, so good! Daniel is praying, heaven is listening, and help is on the way. However, here the plot takes a temporary turn for the worse:

> *"But the prince of the kingdom of Persia withstood me twenty-one days; and behold, Michael, one of the chief princes, came to help*

27

me, for I had been left alone there with the kings of Persia." Daniel 10:13

Here are some points to contemplate about this insightful backstage look at prayer.

We are not the only ones involved in spiritual warfare. A realm of angels and demons are in conflict at a level we can only marvel at and be glad we are on the right side. Satan is determined to frustrate the purposes of God. Christians will experience this spiritual wrestling whenever we take part in the "Father's business." We must always remember the battle is not ours. Notice that this transaction involved invisible powers and personalities far beyond our spiritual pay grade. Like Daniel, our part is to pray, then let God have His way. This is a key point that we will expand upon further in our studies.

Prayer is the primary avenue of access to spiritual resources. Please note—Daniel's answer was on the way immediately. This illuminates the vital principle that we have been granted many precious and wonderful promises in scripture, but they often do not seem real or even possible. Pastor Tony Evans once said: "Faith is just acting like what God said is true!"

Satan is consistent, so Daniel was persistent; he did not give up. Even though the answer was delayed, Daniel stayed the course, and we must do the same. Are you praying for the salvation of friends and family? Be sure that you will experience spiritual resistance and delay. Do not give up, and do not grow weary.

Invisible but Powerful

The Bible uses its words wisely when we are told that we wrestle not against flesh and blood but against powers and principalities and against spiritual wickedness in high places. We need to take it seriously. When I was in junior high school, we had an ex-drill sergeant from the Marines who taught wrestling. As a little skinny guy of one hundred pounds, I needed some coaching to have any hope of success. I learned that through hard work and leverage, I could drive larger guys to the ground. "Drive, drive, drive!" is what our coach would yell.

Many people show up and want to be involved in this good fight of faith. They come for the match, but not for hard work on the mat. Wrestling involves commitment and endurance. That is the kind of sacrifice in prayer Daniel displayed, and it paid off.

God is calling us to wrestle. We are not in a contest for our salvation, but we are to stand firm in Jesus Christ in order to avoid the instability of human emotions and reasoning. We are to stand upon the Word of God. Why? Because the flesh wars against your spirit constantly, it is always contrary to the Spirit of God.

First and foremost, you are not wrestling against flesh and blood. The apostle Paul came to the place of understanding that his real battles could be confused by the "fog of war" created by interpersonal human conflict. He knew that the flesh nature of man can never please God or be in harmony with His purposes. So he concluded he would, "Know no man after the flesh."

I believe a lot of times the Devil just stands back and snickers because he gets us tangled up in our horizontal relationships, going the wrong direction and against each other. If he can instigate conflict in the church, he will enjoy the scene while we devour one another.

Paul certainly puts his finger on a huge relational problem that we must come to terms with. When we are consumed by the use of our energies in conflict with brothers and sisters, we will be too distracted and fatigued to take part in the battle that really matters. By observation and experience, Paul came to the conclusion that he would not waste his time and talent on the frustration of trying to win a carnal battle. We too must understand that to win this war, we must attack the source and not the symptom. This means engaging in the right kind of combat.

Not So Friendly Fire

Pat Tillman was an incredible athlete. At both the college and professional level, he could impact a football game. Opposing teams were always aware of his whereabouts. Pat took this passion and ability onto the real battlefield when the events of 9/11 caused him to abandon football for the U.S. Special Forces. When he turned his back on continuing his lucrative pro-football career, the media marveled at the sacrifice he displayed.

At the same time, Tillman's brother, Kevin, turned down a pro-baseball contract. On May 31, 2002, both Kevin and Pat were inducted into the U.S. Army and served alongside each other. Deployed to Afghanistan as an elite Army Ranger, Pat Tillman exhibited a remarkable level of sacrifice and commitment to his beliefs. What happened next was a tragedy of epic proportions.

On patrol in the mountains of Afghanistan, his unit mistakenly came under heavy fire from another allied unit and Pat Tillman was killed, not by the enemy, but by so-called "friendly fire."

It is an unavoidable fact from the battlefield, in each war, a certain percentage of casualties will be suffered from friendly forces. The official term is *amicicide,* the murder of a friend. Very often, a series of tragic miscalculations results in soldiers from the same side being targeted and attacked. Grief over the loss of a loved one in combat is overwhelming, but it is unthinkable that this loss could be caused by the accidental attack of our own army.

Doing the Devil's Work

It is hard to imagine anything worse than unintended attack from your own side, but it happens—when the fire is intentional. This is not as uncommon as we might think. In Vietnam, unpopular officers of a unit were sometimes killed by fragmentation grenades, resulting in the term *fragging.* Hundreds of cases of possible fragging incidents were reported during the controversial Vietnam War. Because of the nature of death by grenade, fragging is a difficult charge to prove, though there are instances of U.S. soldiers being convicted of this crime.

Attacking Our Mission Field

In the days following Jesus taking Peter, James, and John to the Mount of Transfiguration, the disciples engaged in a series of classic failures. Perhaps none is more blatant than a request to call fire down from heaven on a Samaritan village that refused to welcome Jesus.

31

And when His disciples James and John saw this, they said, "Lord, do You want us to command fire to come down from heaven and consume them, just as Elijah did?" But He turned and rebuked them, and said, "You do not know what manner of spirit you are of. For the Son of Man did not come to destroy men's lives, but to save them. And they went to another village.
Luke 9:54-56

Now that is a divine rebuke. And it points out just how far off task followers of Jesus can drift, and how quickly. These men had the benefit of high and holy intelligence briefings, and yet in quick order they were ready to destroy their mission field! Our marching orders in the Great Commission are clear, and they don't include expending ammunition and energy on the wrong enemy.

Friction Among Friends

The next issue may seem like a minor event in light of the problems created by friendly fire and fragging we have been considering, but internal friction can do serious damage within the church.

When we have our vertical relationship grounded with God, we will find that our priorities will be clear despite the battle raging around us. However, if we are confused and engaged in quarreling and fighting other soldiers for rank and power, our efforts will be wasted. The followers of Jesus learned this lesson the hard way. Time and again they would jockey for position, seeking to be prominent. Sometimes they argued among themselves; other times, they asked Jesus to promote them; and one time, some disciples actually sent their mother to Jesus! All along the way they were focused on the wrong target.

Then the mother of Zebedee's sons came to Him with her sons, kneeling down and asking something from Him.

And He said to her, "What do you wish?" She said to Him, "Grant that these two sons of mine may sit, one on Your right hand and the other on the left, in Your kingdom." Matthew 20:20-21

Clearly, James and John's mother had been put up to this power play, so we are witnessing the outgrowth of an ongoing issue. When the boys could not accomplish a promotion through maneuvering, they tried other tactics. In any case, this episode underscores the lack of clarity that these men had about what their goals should have been. We, too, need to learn that the enemy is not our brother or sister, but spiritual wickedness in high places.

But avoid foolish and ignorant disputes, knowing that they generate strife. 2 Timothy 2:23

Collateral Damage

If we begin to engage in the proper war, we will have incoming spiritual bombs dropped into our lives by the enemy. When this happens, we aren't the only ones who can be harmed. Our families are often damaged by the explosion. Some of the day-to-day conflicts we find in our families are the result of spiritual opposition. Remember, the goal of Satan is to distract God's people from their proper purpose of giving God glory. If our minds can be filled with trivial pursuits of pride and self-seeking, we are cooperating and leading our loved ones right into a trap. Ask yourself this question: if you are wrestling with people, how will you have time and energy to be involved in productive battle for the kingdom? If you are wrestling against the principalities and power of darkness, you will realize the need for unity among the soldiers of light.

This brings up another point concerning the principle of wrestling—where we are wrestling. In other words, the battlefield. Remember, Paul says that we are wrestling with spiritual hosts of wickedness in heavenly places.

We have already noted there is a physical realm that we live in; there's also a spiritual realm that exists simultaneously along with the physical world.

Sometimes we think, "Well, I've got to go on a retreat someplace to actually experience the spiritual." This was a practice of early Christians who sought out monasteries to avoid the worldly, in order to engage in the spiritual. What many found was that their flesh and the enemy were able to follow them to the most remote location! No, the geography of our bodies is not the issue; it is the location of our heart in relation to God that will determine if we are successful soldiers.

Welcome to the Real World War
The story of mankind is stained by the blood of battle. In the course of six millennia of recorded history, precious

few years have seen true peace on earth. The Roman Empire brought into being what was called the *Pax Romana*, the "peace of Rome." This was a two hundred year period between the reign of Augustus and the death of Marcus Aurelius. The use of the word *peace* in this case may be misleading. While this period exemplified Rome at its prime, the lack of war was enjoyed only because of Rome's brutal enforcement of its laws and the relentless suppression of opposition by the legions.

Until the Prince of Peace returns to reign, this world will be at war. But even the awful scope of world wars is not the real story. Let us recall again—we fight against invisible powers!

The book of Job rips the curtain back briefly and reveals another scene from the cosmic drama in which we are a part.

> *Now there was a day when the sons of God came to present themselves before the LORD, and Satan also came among them. And the LORD said to Satan, "From where do you come?" So Satan answered the LORD and said, "From going to and fro on the earth, and from walking back and forth on it."* Job 1:6-7

That is vital insight into what really has been going on in the world since before time began. The worst conflicts on earth are overshadowed by the dramatic warfare that has been taking place between the forces of God and the plans of Satan. This is the true war for the world, but what is at stake is not land or natural resources, as is the case in man's wars. The battle is for eternal souls.

5

Spiritual Terrorism

*I am the way, the truth, and the life. No man
comes to the Father, but by Me.* —Jesus Christ

In the medieval world there was an interesting
tradition in jousting where a king named the winner,
his champion, as a representative. The most talented
and brave knight in the kingdom was referred to as the
King's Champion. And at times, disputes were settled
by the outcome of a joust. In one instance, the King
of England challenged the King of France to combat
between either two champions or one hundred knights
to determine the outcome of a battle. There is also a *Star
Trek* episode titled "Arena" where Captain Kirk is made
a champion who then battles with a reptilian opponent.
The principle of a representative champion was exactly
what took place when Jesus Christ personally confronted
Satan during the incarnation:

> *For if by the one man's offense death reigned
> through the one, much more those who
> receive abundance of grace and of the gift of*

righteousness will reign in life through the One, Jesus Christ. Romans 5:17

We learn here that just as Adam's failure brought the fall upon all mankind, so the victory of Jesus Christ enabled all to enjoy His reign of eternal life.

The Super Brawl

The life of Jesus was full of huge moments. Let's remember, Jesus spoke the very Word of God. Anytime He entered a situation, God was on the scene in the flesh. We need to consider two events from scripture in our study of spiritual warfare. The first came after a period of forty days of fasting by Jesus. During His temptation in the wilderness, we find a great contrast between the scene Jesus faced and the environment in the Garden of Eden. Adam and Eve had every reason to be content, but they disobeyed God's clear order. Jesus was in a desolate location, weak with hunger, and yet He overcame the Tempter!

These two pivotal events represent initial defeat for mankind and then victory through the Son of Man. Satan may have thought he had triumphed in the Garden of Eden, but when Jesus overcame the temptation in the wilderness, the Prince of Darkness saw God's power on display even through weakness.

Terrorism in High Places

The terrorists of our day do not attack directly against the might and force of the United States, but rather use terror tactics to demoralize and destroy. This approach is also used by Satan. His direct rebellion against heaven failed, and now he is left to utilize other methods such as propaganda, character assassination against God, and sowing fear. To stand firm, the church must stand on God's word and fight the spiritual fight with the appropriate weapons.

For the weapons of our warfare are not carnal but mighty in God for pulling down strongholds, casting down arguments and every high thing that exalts itself against the knowledge of God, bringing every thought into captivity to the obedience of Christ, and being ready to punish all disobedience when your obedience is fulfilled. 2 Corinthians 10:4-6

When we engage spiritual forces of darkness in the spiritual realm, in the heavenly places, we are really at an advantage, not a disadvantage. We do not need to fear the battleground. Remember Jesus said, "I will build my church and the gates of Hell will not prevail against it." In the spiritual sense, if Satan and the principalities are in the heavenly places, then they are coming against the kingdom of God, and there is no future in that!

[Jesus who was] far above all principality and power and might and dominion, every name that is named not only in this age, but also in that which is to come. Ephesians 1:21

We do not have to fear what the Devil schemes; he cannot afflict a child of the kingdom without God's express permission. And when God allows oppression, it is for His ultimate glory. That is what happened with Job; God personally managed the limits of the trial that His servant went through.

Remember this point: Satan needs divine permission to take any action against someone who belongs to God. This should be great comfort.

Knowing What Demons Know

When Jesus cast the demons out of the swine, they complained, "Have you come to torment us before our time?" They knew their judgment was coming, so they tried to postpone it: "So the demons begged Him, saying, 'If You cast us out, permit us to go away into the herd of swine'" (Matthew 8:31).

Next we see an example of a type of suicide insanity, a logic we can only wonder at. When Jesus allowed the demons to go into the pigs, they ran the pigs off the cliff to drown in the water.

We should be sure to note that whatever the Devil does, and whatever these spiritual powers and principalities attempt, however intimidating they might sound, they need the permission of Christ to even move from place to place.

Take heart, saint of God! You can detect the schemes of Satan and boldly overcome them. Victory is yours when you allow the Spirit of God to put your carnal desires in perspective and empower you to master them. Much more than mere survival awaits the Christian who takes God's promises seriously and seeks first the kingdom of God.

Therefore submit to God. Resist the devil and he will flee from you. James 4:7

God desires that His children lead lives worthy of spiritual royalty. This does not mean arrogance but assuming spiritual privileges granted only to His family. Remember though, the greatest in this kingdom are servants of all. Nonetheless, our inheritance of spiritual authority is a massive gift we receive upon conversion. Though the keys to the kingdom belong to us, God progressively opens doors based on our responsibility and maturity.

Are you a person who is totally, utterly dependent on God; who has no confidence in himself or herself? Then you are in a place of power! This is another paradox of the kingdom. Imagine a person on his or her knees, eyes closed, hands clasped. Now, this is just one of several positions for prayer that we find illustrated in scripture, but it makes a very strong point. From a human perspective, this kneeling person is vulnerable and powerless. But from heaven's viewpoint and in spiritual reality, this praying saint is a dynamo of power, able to access the very resources of heaven.

Plugged In and Powered Up

Finally, my brethren, be strong in the Lord and in the power of His might. Ephesians 6:10

The power of His might represents being filled with the Holy Spirit. This means coming to God daily and saying, "Lord, I need You. Fill me with Your power. Fill me with Your Spirit. I cannot do this apart from You." That prayer will always be answered if we are sincere. Jesus understands. That is why He said, "I am the vine, you are the branches, and apart from Me, you can do nothing."

Now, it would seem there are some things we can do on our own. I can hit a baseball without Jesus. I can go bowling without Him. I'm being facetious, but the bottom line is, some activities in our lives are put on auto-pilot, and yet our every breath is in His hands. What a fantastic God we serve!

Plans for Peter

In Luke, Jesus painted a vivid picture of Peter being run through the mill by Satan and destroyed. The Devil would like to sift you like wheat, just as he planned to do to Peter. We can be sure Peter was alarmed by this breaking news from Jesus, and did not want to go through this process. He must have been relieved to hear Jesus say that He was intervening.

> *And the Lord said, "Simon, Simon! Indeed, Satan has asked for you, that he may sift you as wheat, but I have prayed for you that your faith should not fail."* Luke 22:31-32 (a)

So, Peter could take heart and know that even though the Devil had his address, Jesus had his back! Ultimately, Satan wishes our total destruction. This point is tragically dramatized in the life of Judas Iscariot. Here was a man with first-person access to the Son of God. Judas witnessed the miracles and heard the actual Word of God spoken, and yet, Satan found a place in his heart. This stronghold was used to drive Judas to the betrayal of Jesus. This sobering story should warn us and remind us that Satan is not an enemy to be taken lightly. Thank God we have a Savior who is stronger still!

Staying When We Should Be Going

The enemy never rests, never stops, and can only be resisted in the power of the Spirit. King David learned this lesson with painful results. One year, at the time when kings go out to battle, David sent out Joab and his servants while he remained in Jerusalem.

And shortly after this, his idle time led him astray.

In the spring, at the time when kings go off to war, Joab led out the armed forces. 1 Chronicles 20:1 (a)

As we see here, in the spring the king of Israel typically led his troops into battle. War was part of the lifestyle of Israel's kings. Very often a near constant state of war existed between Israel and its neighboring countries. Not much has changed!

In this case of Israel's most famous king, David, who had won so many victories at the head of Israel's army, chose to sit this one out. Perhaps he thought he had done enough. Maybe he was burned out on battle, and decided he was due for an extended holiday. In any case, it was a poor decision because David learned that war does not rest because we do. When David left his place at the head of the column of soldiers, he stepped into the cross hairs of a spiritual battle that would leave an indelible mark on his life. This episode of intrigue involved David's adultery with Bathsheba and the death of her husband Uriah.

The story tragically tells us that David plotted so her husband would not find out; he put her husband in the front lines in the battle and he was killed. So, David was guilty of adultery and murder. Bathsheba became pregnant with his child, and he tried to cover it up.

Let's take time to focus on the "when" of what took place. What happens in the springtime? Everybody gets loose. It's warm, the sun's shining, life is good. The feeling of love is in the air. I think David just said, "It's tough being king. I deserve a break. I've been at war all of this time. I'm just going to kick back."

He took his armor off and that is when the enemy tempted and deceived him. Do you see that David voluntarily disarmed himself? It can be the same way with us—in the spring of our lives, we must be careful, because the enemy will come in and deceive us. That is when we are often the most susceptible to the soothing sounds of deception. We are tempted to lay our armor aside and stay behind and let someone else fight the battle, or let somebody else pray, or let somebody else preach. This is when our ears become dull to the voice of God and our heart grows insensitive. This incident was not typical of David's life, but tragically he carried the scars of this lost encounter to the grave.

One Size Does Not Fit All

Earlier in his career, David learned a valuable lesson when he realized he couldn't wear Saul's armor. And that goes for us—you can't wear somebody else's armor. God's armor is custom-fitted for you. In other words, you have to come as an individual and be fitted.

Of course, the basics of our protection are identical in terms of the gift of salvation and the gospel. But when it comes to our ability to use the sword, for example, some are teachers, others preachers, and still others are not gifted to speak publicly. God does not want us comparing ourselves among ourselves, because this is not wise or productive.

Be sure to understand that God wants an individual and personal relationship with each of His children. He does not have assembly-line armor that is one-size-fits-all. You are being uniquely prepared for what lies ahead. Your Father can see what battles you will face, and now you are being equipped with exactly what is required to meet and overcome the obstacles that you will encounter. Nothing comes into your life except what is personally approved by your loving heavenly Father.

> *"For I know the thoughts that I think toward you, says the Lord. Thoughts of peace and not of evil to give you a hope and a future. Then you will call upon me and go and pray to me and I will listen to you, and you will seek me and find me when you search for me with all your heart. I will be found by you, says the Lord, and I will bring you back from your captivity."* Jeremiah 29:11-14a

Anxiety and worry can bind and paralyze anyone. Jesus is here today to set you free and bring you out of captivity. Perhaps you've laid aside your armor. It's time to come out of the pit of despair, put on the whole armor of God and assume your position on the battlefield. Your brothers and sisters at arms are ready to welcome you into the fray.

A Quick Lesson from Job

Here is a never-fail set of marching orders that come from the life of Job. He was a man who could have easily made an excuse to go AWOL and spiral into depression and desertion. He did not, and you must not. Job adopted an attitude that could not be overcome; he was determined to serve God, even if it meant losing his life.

The wise believer will remain alert through each season of life. There is no retirement from the principles of spiritual engagement, regardless of our past spiritual triumphs or failures. We must remain vigilant until that perfect day.

6

Staging for Battle

The triumphant Christian does not fight for victory; he celebrates a victory already won.
—Captain Reginald Wallis

Jesus was very blunt about the condition of the religious leaders He encountered:

You are of your father the devil, and the desires of your father you want to do. He was a murderer from the beginning, and does not stand in the truth, because there is no truth in him. When he speaks a lie, he speaks from his own resources, for he is a liar and the father of it. John 8:44

That's strong but not overstated, because the problem with the Pharisees was severe and profound; despite their posturing, they did not know God. They honored Him with their lips, but their heart was far from Him. Clearly Jesus was not interested in winning friends or influencing people. Jesus is always devoted to telling the truth, and that is what he did here. Satan is, in fact, an enemy of our souls and he is serious about his mission. He was, as Jesus sums him up, a murderer from the beginning. He does not stand in the truth because there is no truth in him; he is a liar and the father of lies. His agenda is to kill, steal, and to destroy. This is the leader of our opposition. He'll never come to the peace table—his fate is sealed and his doom is certain.

Let us be sure to carefully understand the articles of war. Anyone in the church of Jesus Christ is expected to serve as a soldier of truth. Our assignment is to be light in the world; to illuminate Jesus Christ as the only way of salvation. That task automatically declares war on the kingdom of darkness. "Oh, but that's not what I signed up for. I signed up for 'The Love Boat.'" God said, "I called you to a battleship." Perhaps you are thinking, "When is the pool going to be open? When is my time for that massage and where is the sauna? Can somebody point it out? Where's the buffet? Where are the waiters?" But God says, "Man your battle stations."

God is calling us to fight, often in hand-to-hand combat. We are not in a contest for our salvation. But we need to stand firm in Jesus Christ. We need not be swayed back and forth by our human reasoning and emotions, but we must stand upon the Word of God.

A Relentless Enemy

Though Satan is conquered and defeated, that does not mean he is done causing havoc. World War II formally ended in 1945 when Japan conceded defeat, yet Japanese soldiers continued fighting long after the war was over. Some, on remote Pacific islands, continued hostilities for years. That is how Satan is; instead of laying down arms, he is picking up the pace. We do not need to analyze this demonic logic, but we cannot afford to be ignorant of it. Satan does understand that God has *blessed us with every spiritual blessing in the heavenly places with Christ* (Ephesians 1:3). The forces of hell are understandably terrified of our potential and will do anything to prevent us from reaching it.

Resistance Training

What purpose does it serve for this conflict to continue if the outcome is a foregone conclusion? One answer is you! God knows character is not refined when we are at ease. Discipline seldom increases when we are on vacation but it does increase when we are forced to face resistance. Learn the lesson of the weight room—no one builds muscles lying by the pool. Growth comes from resisting the force of the weights.

So it is with your "spiritual muscles"—they don't grow unless they are forced to flex during sets of repetitive lifting. Resistance training also improves bodily immune systems, boosts energy, and improves attitude. These bodily benefits are mirrored by what takes place when a Christian is spiritually fit. Lethargy is an enemy of vitality and spiritual health. Consider this strong warning against complacency:

> *Moab has been at ease from his youth; he has settled on his dregs, and not been emptied from vessel to vessel, nor has he gone into captivity. Therefore his taste remained in him, and his scent has not changed.* Jeremiah 48:11

A life of ease and predictability leads to a soft soldier! Challenged lives can become changed lives. There is a reason why new recruits to the military are sent through rigorous training.

Another reason God allows Satan to afflict and harass is so that you will be motivated to call upon His name. Without war, you would not have the opportunity to declare God's name or depend on His strength, and you would have no reason to use the spiritual equipment you have been provided with.

And so, for now the war continues. It is time to get the armor on.

7

Aware and Alert

There is no neutral ground in the universe; every square inch, every split second is claimed by God, and counter-claimed by Satan.
—C.S. Lewis

Since we are facing a super-intelligent horde of satanic beings who happen to be invisible, we need some serious help. And that is just what God has provided through spiritual armor.

For though we walk in the flesh, we do not war according to the flesh, for the weapons of our warfare are not of the flesh, but divinely powerful for the pulling down of strongholds.
2 Corinthians 10:3-4

Human strength is no match in this battle—alone, we are over-matched. Spiritual warfare cannot be met with natural weapons. Imagine Paul in his Roman prison cell writing his letter to the Ephesian church. From his forced imprisonment, Paul had a chance to carefully inventory the armament carried by a Roman soldier. With this view, he went about describing six vital pieces of armor and made the application to what is available to each Christian. As we go through the operating instructions for each of the pieces of armor, we will find that they are uniquely suited for our needs. God's all-volunteer army is always open to new recruits. A recruiting advertisement from heaven would be this:

> *For the eyes of the Lord run to and fro throughout the whole earth, to show Himself strong on behalf of those whose heart is loyal to Him.* 2 Chronicles 16:9 (a)

Blessed Are the Flexible

Aware, alert and flexible, those are three positive qualities a good soldier will adopt.

It is a remarkable privilege to be able to invest ourselves in service of the King. I am constantly amazed by His willingness to use me and anyone else who sincerely seeks to serve.

Here is an example of learning to be flexible and allowing the Lord to open doors to take the gospel of peace wherever we go. One time, before we left for an outreach in Mexico, we prayed, "God give us souls. God give us souls." The first night we had a tent meeting. It was a wonderful night, but no one really responded to the gospel. The next day we were going out to a place called Felipe, a community that only about six months before finally got electricity. It had rained the night before, and the journey up there was treacherous, as we wound up muddy, mountain roads, but it led to a beautiful valley. The people lived by farming and shepherding in this gorgeous area, but they lived in abject poverty.

We were going to do a clothing distribution, but there was still very little response and we considered leaving. One of the pastors encouraged us to be patient and before long, the people began to come to us. They were ragged, but beautiful and humble folks. We had probably sixty or so people standing around. We had intended to move on to the next village. Preaching was not in the plan; we were just dropping the clothes off and then we were going off to do another clothing distribution. Yet, as the people gathered and gave us their attention, I began to share the gospel through an interpreter. And we gave an opportunity to receive Christ as Lord and Savior.

You must understand that this is a very religious area. In fact, we were told that only one woman was a known Christian in that area. And she walked three hours every Sunday to Santa Clara to visit her father's church. There was no shortage of religion, but the people were not born again.

The response was immediate; I think about everybody that was there ended up praying with me. Now, we didn't plan that, but God had. We were looking in another place, yet God gave us souls, but not where we thought.

I'll never forget what one lady said: "Why would you come to the end of the earth, a place totally forgotten by time?" I was so moved by her comment and I said, "Because God hasn't forgotten you, and Jesus loves you."

We must remember that there is not a God-forsaken location on earth. There may be church-forsaken places, but the gospel will reach all the earth, and then the end will come.

This is such a wonderful picture of God's faithfulness. If we are willing to be bold when God makes the appointment, we will see Him move. Remember, the Great Commission was His idea!

Portable Power

As we take inventory of the spiritual weaponry we have been issued, we must be careful to note an important distinction in the six pieces of armor listed in Ephesians chapter six. The first three—our belt, breastplate, and shoes—are always in place. This is why Paul says we *have* each of these items. However, there is a shift when we come to the second batch of armor. Regarding the shield, helmet, and sword, Paul tells us to *take* them. We must actively add these elements of warfare to our daily wardrobe. Upon reflection, this shows us that truth, righteousness, and the gospel are always in place in our lives; they are standard equipment for the Christian. However, we take the shield, helmet, and sword as needed; they are available to us as the situation requires.

Having and Taking

A good illustration of this point would be a baseball player. They always have their uniform and cleats on, but they pick up their glove or bat as warranted by the moment. In the same way, we raise our shield of faith when attacks come, and we pick up the sword of the spirit and remind ourselves of scripture to combat doubt or depression. This is one way of taking up our tools of spiritual warfare.

Soldiers slept with their swords nearby; similarly, we need to know where our weapons are at all times because a tremendous battle is raging in the spiritual realm. Forces beyond our sight and understanding have been warring for longer than we can imagine. From our earth-bound perspective, we get only a glimpse of the overall battle. We can let our imaginations ponder the revelation of scripture concerning God and Satan, but what we are mainly concerned with is our personal piece of the war. Basically, we should fully involve ourselves in the battle in front of us. When we see our calling in Christ as an assignment from our Commander in Chief, our daily conflicts are elevated to an entirely new level. How amazing that God has allowed the war against His name, honor, and position to take place so that we can witness His power.

8

The Belt of Truth

You have established a new relationship with the powers of darkness. Whatever you were before you were a Christian... you are now a sworn foe of the legions of hell. Have no delusions about their reality or their hostility, but do not fear them. The God inside you terrifies them. They cannot touch you, let alone hurt you, but they can still seduce, and they will try. They will also oppose you as you obey Christ. ... if you are serious about Christ being your Lord and God, you can expect opposition.
— John White

Therefore take up the whole armor of God, that you may be able to withstand in the evil day, and having done all, to stand. Stand therefore, having girded your waist with truth, having put on the breastplate of righteousness, and having shod your feet with the preparation of the gospel of peace; above all, taking the shield of faith with which you will be able to quench

all the fiery darts of the wicked one. And take the
helmet of salvation, and the sword of the Spirit,
which is the word of God; Ephesians 6:13-17

Six pieces of armor make up the offensive and defensive weaponry that is detailed in our study of this portion of scripture. Each item has a specific purpose for the spiritual soldier, and, as we have noted, further examination reveals an interesting distinction between those pieces that the soldier has, and those that he takes up. This reminds us that our warfare does not take place as we are wandering nonchalantly through the battle; we must willfully and consciously *take up* arms.

First, let's have an examination of the tools of war that are fixtures.

A Soldier in Full View

Paul's familiarity with soldiers of the Roman army allowed him to develop the point that just as these soldiers required physical armor to fight their wars, Christians need spiritual armor to successfully fight theirs. For anyone growing up in a Roman province, soldiers would have been virtually everywhere, because Rome made its presence felt. Now, up close and chained to a soldier, Paul saw that each piece of Roman armor had a clear relationship to our own spiritual defense and offense.

The life of a soldier of Rome was not an easy one. The Roman philosophy of warfare was revolutionary and built the Empire. Legionaries were trained hard and disciplined well. They were expected to march twenty miles a day under a seventy-pound pack. Soldiers had to be able to swim rivers after a forced march, and then conduct brutal hand-to-hand combat. There was no transportation department in ancient Rome! It was the army that built a quarter million miles of the famed Roman Roads. A Roman legion was a powerful unit to behold. Loyal, determined, and well-armed, they conquered what was set before them.

This would have been the image Paul had in mind as he visualized the spiritual warfare that Christian soldiers would face. Early evangelists took advantage of the roads Rome had built to carry the gospel worldwide. They faced frequent hazards and eventually endured persecution from Rome itself. Their commander, however, was above even Caesar and their kingdom was not of this world. These believers counted the cost and found the cross worthy of their lives. We must do the same.

Armor of Light

And do this, knowing the time, that now it is high time to awake out of sleep; for now our salvation is nearer than when we first believed. The night is far spent, the day is at hand. Therefore let us cast off the works of darkness, and let us put on the armor of light. Let us walk properly, as in the day, not in revelry and drunkenness, not in lewdness and lust, not in strife and envy. But put on the Lord Jesus Christ, and make no provision for the flesh, to fulfill its lusts. Romans 13:11-14

The scene is set. God's forces are engaged in a great battle against an enemy determined to hinder the church. Satan has a no-holds-barred strategy, yet he must conduct his campaign under the parameters set by the Lord Himself. This must be frustrating, but we have no sympathy for the Devil. The armor of light—what a wonderful gift we have been given to equip us for the war that lies ahead. Armor of light is ideal because we fight a dark spiritual enemy.

Paul admonishes the church to also put on the Lord Jesus Christ; that is, to assume His identity as we maintain our personality. What Paul anticipates is the decreasing expression of our fallen carnality. This requires the death of the old nature as we pick up our cross daily and follow Jesus.

When soldiers complete their training and are ready for the battlefield, they are issued the weapons equivalent with their training and assignments. Let's take a look at each piece of armor that God has provided for us. We must know how to wear and use each in order to assume the spiritual authority we have been given.

Holding It All Together: The Belt of Truth
...Stand therefore, having girded your loins with truth...

Charles Spurgeon said,

"Nothing makes a man so virtuous as belief of the truth. A lying doctrine will soon beget a lying practice. A man cannot have an erroneous belief without by-and-by having an erroneous life. I believe the one thing naturally begets the other."

Nothing but the Truth

Truth comes first. Everything in the Christian life is held together by truth. It sets us free and holds our world together, providing clarity and certainty for our mission. The Roman soldiers wore this special belt around their waist; all the other parts of the armor connected to the belt. When the soldier started to run, his armor was stabilized by his belt. The belt was the core piece of a soldier's uniform. It was not decorative, but vitally functional.

The rest of our armor will not hold together if we do not maintain a lifelong dedication to the truth. Current conventional wisdom says that truth is relative, not absolute, and that each person experiences and defines truth in their own way. Nothing could be further from, well, the truth! Truth is not defined by humans; it is mandated by God.

Jesus said, *"I am the way, the truth, and the life."* That is a bold statement, not open to personal interpretation.

Truth distinguishes the church from darkness, because Satan is the father of lies (John 8:44). Unless our waist is firmly girded by absolute biblical truth, we will be subject to the slick lies of the enemy.

Function First

The armor that Roman soldiers wore served various purposes. This type of armor was often made of a finely looped chain linked together. Since it was a loose garment, it required a belt to help it fit tight against the body. The belt also was where the sword would be sheathed.

As Paul patterned his illustration after the Roman soldiers he studied, he wanted his readers to know truth holds everything together, so this belt was a basic but crucial part of the wardrobe; everything was connected to it. The same can be said of truth in the Christian life. Our walk falls apart if we depart from the truth.

Sanctify them by Your truth. Your word is truth.
John 17:17

For a belt to be effective and accomplish its purposes, it must be one continuous piece.

And just as a belt goes around the waist, truth must surround each soldier. This is one of the major distinctions that sets Christians apart from others who pursue virtue. There are those who seek honor through literature, poetry, or philosophy, but relative truth is no truth at all. It is only Christian warriors who can take confidence that they walk in total truth.

Tighten Up

Be sure to note that each piece of armor compliments the whole; if one piece were missing the soldier would be badly hindered. The belt in particular is so central that no soldier would go into battle without it.

We are told, "Gird up the loins of your mind." This implies tucking in long garments to be ready to move quickly. The soldier needed to be ready for action at a moment's notice. This was accomplished by pulling up the fabric and tucking the excess material snugly into the belt. Now there's nothing flapping and no loose tunic to trip you up.

Therefore gird up the loins of your mind, be sober,
and rest your hope fully upon the grace that is to
be brought to you at the revelation of Jesus Christ.
1 Peter 1:13

Spiritually, this tells us to secure any thoughts or habits that will stumble us or impede our progress. A Christian soldier must be agile, and loose thinking can be a snare.

The world seems so certain there are no absolutes, only equally valid opinions. This false belief is necessary for ignoring any possible accountability to God. Truth declares that there are eternal and unchanging absolutes, and that each person will answer for his actions. As Christian soldiers, we know that there is truth, and that it is definite and not negotiable.

Guarding What We Value
We have all watched an armored truck with guards taking their job with utmost seriousness. They consider the money being transported to be worthy of the possible use of deadly force. An armored vehicle is designed with great care to protect its contents. The same is true of banks and repositories of worldly treasures. Vaults, safes, and alarms are engineered to guarantee a safe place for deposit of worldly valuables.

Truth is a great treasure entrusted to the church. How much more, then, should the church guard the truth that has been delivered to us? We need to be on guard because Satan comes first with a spirit of error and then a wave of persecution. He poisons the mind of man, then he fills hearts with hatred for heaven. The magnificent truth we have been granted has caused saints to abandon homes, surrender possessions, and put physical well-being in grave jeopardy. And all of this has been offered with a sacrificial joy, not counting the cost.

Truth will keep you together when all around you is falling apart. It will open your eyes when others are blinded by deceit. Above all, this path will lead you to Jesus, because He is the truth.

9

The Breastplate
OF RIGHTEOUSNESS

Because God is holy, acceptance with Him on the ground of creature doings is utterly impossible. A fallen creature could sooner create a world than produce that which would meet the approval of infinite Purity. Can darkness dwell with Light? Can the Immaculate One take pleasure in "filthy rags" (Isa. 64:6)? The best that sinful man brings forth is defiled. A corrupt tree cannot bear good fruit. God would deny Himself, vilify His perfections, were He to account as righteous and holy that which is not so in itself; and nothing is so which has the least stain upon it contrary to the nature of God. But blessed be His name, that which His holiness demanded His grace has provided in Christ Jesus our Lord. Every poor sinner who has fled to Him for refuge stands "accepted in the Beloved" (Eph. 1:6). —A.W. Pink

...Having put on the breastplate of righteousness...

Modern physical trainers have learned more and more about the importance of aerobic training to provide cardiovascular fitness. In the spiritual realm, our heart is the intersection of our mind, emotions, will, and conscience. This sensitive zone must be protected at all costs. While wounds to our extremities can be painful, a wounded heart will be fatal.

The breastplate was the central item of the armor worn by a Roman soldier, protecting the organs of the torso. A strong breastplate became the foundation of his defensive weaponry; to enter battle with the chest exposed would have been to invite a terminal injury. Roman armor acknowledged this fact by providing a breastplate made of metal or tough animal hide. Some were even cast in metal in the form of the ideal male physique.

So vital was this armor that Paul equated it to our standing before God. *Righteousness* means "right standing," the permission granted for sinful man to approach and enjoy the very presence of God. The Lord is perfect and holy; sinful man is the exact opposite.

> *But we are all like an unclean thing, and all our righteousness are like filthy rags; we all fade as a leaf, and our iniquities, like the wind, have taken us away.* Isaiah 64:6

Constant Protection

Our strong breastplate provides constant protection against condemnation, because righteousness assures us that we have right standing before God. This is not the result of our own goodness or any accumulation of points with God; we are granted access before the throne only by the shared right standing that Jesus gives us. Therefore, we can keep a pure heart by remaining sheltered behind the breastplate of righteousness as it remains attached to our belt of truth.

The Dagger of Failure

Paul correlates the breastplate with righteousness in the Christian life, so we must carefully define what this term means.

> *There is therefore no condemnation to those who are in Christ Jesus, who do not walk according to the flesh, but according to the Spirit.* Romans 8:1

Failure can be a spiritual dagger plunged into our innermost being, leading to guilt, and opening the way for self-condemnation.

One of the most powerful revelations in the Christian walk can come when we realize how thorough the forgiveness we enjoy really is. Guilt and shame are powerful tools of our enemy that must be repelled if we are to walk in freedom and joy. Condemnation can come as a quick and damaging attack when we fail; this onslaught must be met immediately by boasting in the Lord and His great gift of righteousness.

Freedom Awaits

Great liberation awaits anyone who grasps the freedom granted by God's grace. Since nothing can separate a believer from God's love, grace means that Christians live in a constant state of forgiveness. Though salvation is immediate upon confession and the willingness to repent, a three-part chain reaction is set in motion for the born again believer in Jesus Christ. Justification, sanctification, and glorification—these are the elements of salvation. First the past is justified, it is just as if we have never sinned; then in the present we are being sanctified, which means separated from sin. On the day we enter the eternal state, we will be glorified—removed from the presence of sin; this is the great hope of all believers. Biblical hope is not a flimsy thing; it is a definite expectancy of a forthcoming event. We hope in salvation in an absolute way.

When we are righteous, we know that we can come freely before the throne of grace. God's commandments are pure and perfect. By contrast, lawlessness is sin, and sin is the opposite of righteousness. Standing before God creates a desire to please Him. Obedience protects us from the contaminating effects of unrighteousness, and when we do fail, our freedom to approach and receive grace produces a perfect cycle of liberty. Liberty breeds confidence, and this leads to holy boldness.

Here's a fascinating fact from the prophet Isaiah: God Himself puts on righteousness as a breastplate. Perhaps Paul was inspired by this scripture as he crafted the illustration of a Roman soldier and spiritual weapons:

For He put on righteousness as a breastplate, And a helmet of salvation on His head; He put on the garments of vengeance for clothing, And was clad with zeal as a cloak. Isaiah 59:17

68

A Wrong Religion

Elsewhere in his writings, Paul gives us further explanation about this piece of armor.

> *But let us who are of the day be sober, putting on the breastplate of faith and love, and as a helmet the hope of salvation.* 1 Thessalonians 5:8

Righteousness is the foundation of all we do in the Christian life, because our standing before God must be blameless; there can be no confusion about this fact. Recall that the breastplate was one of the pieces that was not taken off; it is a constant fact of life for the Christian soldier. Wearing righteousness requires a life-long commitment to standing before God, secure in the knowledge of our forgiveness.

Therefore, it is very important that we understand the need to reject any other promise of right standing with God other than what He provides. Jesus spent a good deal of time and energy making it clear to strongly religious persons that they were on the wrong path— one that did not lead to right standing with God.

> *For I say to you, that unless your righteousness exceeds the righteousness of the scribes and Pharisees, you will by no means enter the kingdom of heaven.* Matthew 5:20

That is a strong condemnation of even the faintest hope that we can earn salvation on our own terms or in our own power. It is only when we surrender our own corrupt righteousness that we can enjoy what God intended all along. This is a hard and humbling lesson that we all must learn. When this truth is digested, we are prepared to be clothed with heavenly provision. Many of the most prestigious and powerful religious figures of Jesus' day could not accept this fact; they were certain that their brand of keeping the Law of Moses would certainly lead to God's acceptance. Wrong.

If you have not ended this controversy in your own heart and mind, please pause and do so here and now. There can be no debate. You will be unable to successfully enter into spiritual warfare until you surrender in the battle between your ego and God's grace!

Confident to the Core

In the Puritan classic, *The Christian in Complete Armor*, William Gurnall wrote, "A dead soldier will do as much good as a dead-hearted one, paralyzed with anxiety; his heart is attacked and he is murdered while he is still alive."

A soldier who is certain of his standing in his heart will march confidently into battle. If a soldier is fearful of his or her safety, or guilty over past behavior, they will be unlikely to head to the front lines and perform well. Boldness in battle is the result of a full inventory of armor, firmly in place. And for us, that inventory must include the breastplate of righteousness.

With the belt of truth and a breastplate of righteousness, we are ready to consider our footwear and have traction for future action.

10

Feet of Peace

The church in the West today presents too easy a target for Satan. We do not believe we are at war. We do not know where the battleground is located, and, in spite of our weapons, they are neither loaded nor aimed at the right target. We are unaware of how vulnerable we are. We are better fitted for a parade than for an amphibious landing.   —Ed Silvoso

...Having shod your feet with the preparation of the gospel of peace...

We have seen the paintings of the American Revolutionary Army wintering at Valley Forge. They depict shivering soldiers huddling through the frozen Pennsylvania winter. Notably, many of the soldiers were not wearing shoes, but rags wrapped around their feet. George Washington's army suffered greatly from the lack of suitable shoes. There have been other cases in history where armies were defeated because of insufficient footwear.

The *shoes of the gospel of peace* are the third item of armor and the last of the three worn at all times, every day. If a soldier was to stand firm, he certainly needed reliable footwear.

The gospel of Jesus Christ transports believers to where they need to be, confident in their standing in God's army. Our peace *with* God allows us to take confident steps with rest in our souls.

A Roman Revolution

The Roman approach to battle revolutionized warfare, and none of their improvements to ancient combat was more basic than footwear. Many armies went to war barefoot or in flimsy sandals. The Romans understood that firm footing was a huge advantage for their troops. Without it, soldiers could not get leverage in hand-to-hand combat or move quickly on uneven terrain.

Therefore the Romans depended on a thick, hobnail style of boot that came around their foot and strapped on securely. On the bottom of the boots, little pieces of metal protruded like track spikes giving them a grip on the ground.

How appropriate, then, that Paul comments on the need for Christian soldiers to have their feet shod with the gospel of peace. Everywhere we go, every step we take, the gospel goes with us! The Good News of Jesus Christ paves the way for our progress, and each step in our path is guided by the gospel. The traction that Christian soldiers enjoy is based on the firm strength and protection that the gospel provides. We do not slip as we march under the orders of our Commander in Chief.

Roman footwear gave them a huge advantage against their opponents. Their cleats provided leverage in the battle and traction for uphill or downhill travel. The same is true for our spiritual footwear; whether fighting or facing uneven ground, the great gospel message of peace levels out our journey.

The gospel does bring peace, and how peace is needed in the world. We, who were at war with God, are no longer enemies with Him. Peace with God comes first, but there is more—the peace *of* God. It is possible to be forgiven and enjoy the fruits of salvation without walking in the peace that passes understanding. This is the promise Paul brought in a different letter, and this is the marvelous promise that we can both enjoy and offer to those still in conflict with God.

Barefoot Soldiers?

Study of the Roman legions under Caesar reveals that these soldiers were expected to endure long marches because the Empire was far flung. History also shows that wars could be won or lost because of the mobility of the armies involved.

Picture a fully-armed soldier, prepared for war, but barefoot; that wouldn't work.

A shoeless soldier would often run into trouble on a march or in the heat of battle. But proper footwear allowed him to step freely and without fear as they turned their full attention to the battle at hand.

Paul found protection and strength in the knowledge of what God's gospel meant for him and for the others he shared it with. His footing was sure and certain, and he was always prepared to take the gospel to the ends of the earth. And God sent him to do just that.

> *And how shall they preach unless they are sent? As it is written: "How beautiful are the feet of those who preach the gospel of peace, who bring glad tidings of good things!"* Romans 10:15

The Greek word translated *gospel* simply means "good news." This is the headline we bring to a world steeped in the opposite. Breaking news is almost always about a disaster, scandal, or tragic event. Despite all human attempts at peace, the daily news reports that this world cannot find the road to peace. How good it is to bring the news that God loves and forgives all the world! This is the message God's people should be eager to share with others. Further, our loving Father has prepared a future that goes beyond our imagination. Now that is good news!

Roman Roads

The Roman roads built by the legions were the construction of a vast network that connected much of the empire. Before this Roman vision materialized, adequate worldwide ground transportation simply was not possible. While Rome planned this system to efficiently move legions and commerce, God had another purpose: A means of moving the gospel to all the world. Paul walked countless miles in delivering the Good News. While transportation and communication have changed in our time, we must also be constantly ready to spread the Good News. Today, our roads are information superhighways, and we must put them to use for the kingdom.

Remember, all things were created for His pleasure.

Though We Walk Through the Shadow of Death
The roads that Roman soldiers walked were far from smooth highways, and the roads they marched on led them to uneven battlefields that were a challenge to traverse. Their footgear made a difference. This is also true of the paths that Christians must take; the preparation of the gospel of peace allows us to cover ground full of painful trials and tribulations.

Our footwear enables us to travel without fear, knowing that what ultimately awaits us is greater than anything we could be called on to endure in this world. And while combat boots carry troops into the teeth of a battle, there is also a time when wisdom calls for moving away from trouble. Mark this point well—when the moment comes to move quickly away from a snare or some temptation, we need to be able to be mobile and agile in our escape. Solid footing will allow us to do just that.

Shoes may not be the most glamorous item in our inventory, but as we've seen, you don't want to go to war without them.

11

The Shield

OF FAITH

*My main ambition in life is to be on the Devil's
most wanted list.* —Leonard Ravenhill

*...Above all, taking the shield of faith with
which you will be able to quench all the fiery
darts of the wicked one...*

Now we come to the first piece of armor in the
sequence that must be willfully picked up for use
by the soldier, the shield of faith. We must *take* the shield
of faith and put it to work.

A Roman legion marching together in unison with
shields up was an awesome sight to behold. Roman
shields were two-and-a-half feet wide and three feet tall.
They were curved and laminated with three layers of
wood strips covered with leather. Because of its slight
curve, the shield was able to deflect attacks without
transferring the full force of the assault to the man
holding it.

The edges of the shield were bound with leather.
The Roman shield was designed to deflect fiery darts

or arrows from the enemy. The army of Rome faced this threat frequently and would often place wet animal hides over their shields to quench the flaming arrows.

If you have seen many western movies, you are certainly familiar with this tactic, because these movies often portrayed flaming arrows used as a weapon against settlers and wagon trains. In the same way, Satan bombards us with a barrage of arrows designed to set our lives aflame with his lies. Left unhindered, this blaze will spread and scar you and those around you.

The shield was the most maneuverable part of the warrior's armor. As such, faith is our response to proven truth and becomes a mobile defense against attacks from any direction.

The just shall live by faith. Habakkuk 2:4 (b)

Faith is the instrument God installs in us to receive from Him. Willpower gets you nowhere near heaven; only faith can.

Faith Defined

Here is a biblical definition of *faith* that clears up some common misconceptions:"the substance of things hoped for, the evidence of things not seen." We find that biblical faith is tangible, and evidence gives the seeker certain proof. Faith is not some vague hope or emotion without any grounding in reality. Again, genuine biblical hope is the certainty we can enjoy concerning something that will inevitably take place. We can consider faith the currency that the economy of heaven functions on as it relates to mankind, because God always honors true faith.

Although faith is based on concrete evidence, this does not mean it comes automatically. We must review the evidence and conclude that God has proved Himself to be authentic and consistent. Then we are in a position to exercise our faith. By definition, a shield guards the soldier. So, while a physical shield protects the warrior bodily, faith can protect our spiritual lives even during difficult trials and dangerous attacks.

A Wilderness Example

Satan is always hurling his fiery darts of fear, doubt, and worry, but a shield absorbs and deflects. When our shield is in position, we are covered. Vulnerability comes when we let our shield down and operate in our own confidence. When we stop believing that God is in control, doubts reign, and fear is set loose in our hearts. Keep your shield up and you will be in position to extinguish the fiery darts that are being flung at you.

A shield, then, is the first line of defense, but it can be an offensive weapon as well. Because the shield moved with the attack, a trained soldier could deflect an incoming blow. In fact, a skilled soldier could fend off an enemy and could also give a stunning shove backwards. This is what Jesus did during His temptation in the wilderness. Satan thought he saw an opening through the weakness of God's Son due to extended fasting. He slyly approached Jesus with clever temptations, only to be shoved back as Jesus quoted the Word of God and deflected the attack. This is a prime example of the shield of faith working effectively to repel a frontal attack.

Working Together, Like Turtles

Since Satan is a liar and a thief, we must be prepared for devious surprise attacks. That's why we need other soldiers to get our backs!

Soldiers of Rome solved the problem of attacks on multiple fronts through the clever use of formations. This creative tactic made use of their large shields. When enemies would fire arrows and other missiles at the army from various angles, the soldiers would close ranks into a rectangular formation called the *testudo,* or "tortoise," formation. The soldiers on the outside used their shields to create a wall around the perimeter. Those in the middle raised their shields over their heads to protect everyone from incoming airborne projectiles. The result was the equivalent of an armored tank and it was formidable. As the Roman army joined its shields together, it became a nearly unstoppable force.

This inventive approach illustrates how the body of Christ can work together in unison to deflect severe attacks and be more effective as a unit than as individuals. Locking shields together, we can march forward knowing there is strength in our unity.

12

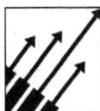

The Helmet
OF SALVATION

*The story of your life is the story of a long
and brutal assault on your heart by the one
who knows what you could be and fears it.*
　　　　　　　　　　　　　—John Eldredge

...And take the helmet of salvation...

We've all read the news stories: "And the crash victim
was killed; he was not wearing a helmet." Whether it
is a motorcycle, skateboard, or bike accident, this is a
common news item. Without a helmet your chances of
survival in a crash dramatically diminish. Worse than that,
in the spiritual scenario, without the helmet of salvation,
your chances of surviving are zero. The Bible repeats the
message clearly—unless we repent, we will all perish.
The helmet of salvation, our fifth piece of equipment,
protects the head which is obviously a vital body area.
There are other vulnerable regions on our bodies, but
nothing happens without the head.

Likewise, without salvation, the rest of the equipment is useless, so protecting the head is primary.

Our minds must be protected so our thought life can filter everything through the grid of our salvation. If we let our thoughts wander and do not take them captive under the supervision of salvation, they will soon be out of control.

Psychiatrists have received the slang nickname "shrinks" because unbalanced people are often subject to an unchecked thought life that torments them. Therefore a goal of psychotherapy can be considered to "shrink" heads and bring them in line. That may work in a limited fashion, but until we submit to God and His prescription for mental health, we will be subject to an unchecked and destructive thought life.

God's Prescription

A large number of American adults are either under some kind of counseling therapy or using mood-altering drugs, or both. God's solution to an unstable mind begins with salvation. No one can really be stable when they are dangling over eternity without assurance of their destination. The great need in each life is for acceptance and love, and that is precisely the message of salvation. God loves us to the extent that He sent His son to die for us. That is the strongest possible expression of His love. The helmet of salvation empowers us to surround our thinking with spiritual truth and confidence, and this leads to sound mental health.

Circle this truth: The gift of God is a sound mind! We need to feed our minds with information from heaven, because this is one way we renew our minds (Romans 12:2). When we put on the helmet of salvation, we restrict Satan's access to our minds, the place where so many battles are won or lost.

It's been said that it's incredible to think that the absence of a helmet can make so much of a difference; that a simple accident can prove fatal without head protection. The proper helmet becomes a life and death issue. Returning to our example of the Roman legions, we can understand why the Romans had developed a very strong defense for attacks to the head.

Though the Romans had special ceremonial helmets that were used in parades to denote rank and standing, when it came time for war, the headgear needed to be functional first. The same is true for our salvation— it must not only be the outward show of plumes and allegiance to Christ that we wear, but real, sturdy, and practical protection for our heads.

Perfect Plan for Fallen People

A helmet protects our brain, the intelligence center, symbolizing that salvation must permeate our total worldview. Everything we think, learn, and come to believe should be filtered through our salvation. Literally, we must take our thoughts captive to Christ if we are to escape the vanity of our own minds. We must be very clear about the definition of salvation. *Salvation* means "to be saved or delivered from the consequences of sin."

For the wages of sin is death, but the gift of God is eternal life in Christ Jesus our Lord. Romans 6:23

Every person who has ever lived has disobeyed God in thought and deed. These sins break the living laws God designed for our welfare. Sin is ugly and repulsive and requires the death sentence for anyone who commits even one.

This is because God's holiness is so perfect that no evil can be tolerated by Him. But God's great grace provided a solution for the human condition. Jesus Christ, through the mercy of God, voluntarily died in our place. Clearly, to be saved, we need a Savior, and that is why Jesus became a man and gave His life as a sacrifice for many; The Perfect One dying for the many that were fallen. God's loving mercy provided the most incredible substitute, Jesus Christ, our Creator, willing to die in our place!

Only God could have devised such a merciful, excellent plan to redeem mankind. Those who take advantage of this offer will spend eternity exploring and praising the wonder of our great God. This is the grand truth that forms a helmet of protection for the saint of God.

For God so loved the world that He gave His only begotten Son, that whoever believes in Him should not perish but have everlasting life. For God did not send His Son into the world to condemn the world, but that the world through Him might be saved. John 3:16-17

Let me repeat, for the sake of absolute clarity: Salvation cannot be earned. It must be received as a gift from God and thus is not something we can accomplish through our actions. It is through the sacrifice of Christ and our coming to the knowledge of the truth, that we accept the free gift of salvation. Grace would not be a gift if it could be earned. We can never do anything to add to or detract from God's wonderful work of salvation.

For by grace you have been saved through faith, and that not of yourselves, it is the gift of God. Ephesians 2:8

When we fail to wear the helmet of salvation, we are unprotected from a bombardment to our mind and emotions. It is no secret that the volume of multi-media has dramatically increased the mass of information we have to deal with. Just one century ago, everything moved much slower. Communication was generally by mail or by word of mouth. Mass media only existed in newspapers and magazines. How things have changed! Now our thought center is under attack from dawn to night. From morning radio or podcast to late night talk show host, we process input from any number of sources. A vast array of opinions, advertisements and other information can assault our faith. We must not allow this data to conform us to the philosophy of this age. This protection is exactly what our helmet accomplishes, filtering out fact from fiction.

A Generation of Screen-agers

The communication revolution is only multiplying addictions to constant information input. A generation of "screen-agers"' does not know life without the Internet. Five-year-olds browse on smart phones and tablets, downloading games at will. It is hard to imagine what the future holds as the techno train races down the tracks. Whatever happens and however quickly it arrives, this much is sure, we will still need to sift all of the information through the facts of salvation.

The Greatest Thought

The human mind is capable of astounding feats. Our brains can calculate complex equations, remember baseball scores from childhood, and simultaneously ponder the meaning of life.

Humankind has put its intellect to staggeringly noble ventures of charity and also devoted its thought life to unspeakable evil. Fearfully and wonderfully made, we must decide how to exercise the great gift of thought.

No more worthy pursuit exists than seeking the face of God and directing our mental capacities toward the knowledge of Him.

And you shall love the LORD your God with all your heart, with all your soul, with all your mind, and with all your strength.' This is the first commandment. Mark 12:30

Almost Ready

Having taken our helmet and shield, we are almost prepared to enter the great struggle before us. With a belt binding us in truth, and a breastplate of holiness, we have shoes leading us on a path of peace paved with the gospel. We can then confidently carry the shield of faith and we must be sure to strap on the helmet of salvation because we are going to need it. Now it's time for the sword of truth.

13

The Sword

OF THE SPIRIT

The mere act of prayer is abhorrent to the forces of evil, and you will find that there will be all kinds of hindrances (depression, doubt, frustrations). Many of those hindrances will have the smell of sulfur smoke about them.
—Steve Brown

...Take the sword of the Spirit, which is the Word of God...

The Roman arsenal contained several styles of swords for various combat strategies. A foot soldier would carry a *gladius*, Latin for "sword," a weapon designed for short-range combat. Sharpened on both edges, this blade was potent when the battle drew close. Its tapered point could even pierce metal. This is the sword that helped make the Roman legion a force to be feared all over the world. But a Roman infantryman would also have a dagger, long-range spears, and perhaps some darts for throwing. Charioteers and cavalry were armed with a longer and more slender sword to provide an advantage from a mounted position. But it was the short sword that helped make the Roman army so fearsome. The Romans were experts in adopting sword designs that would create advantages in combat.

It is not an exaggeration to say that the introduction of the Roman sword onto the battlefield shifted the balance of power in the world. This was the weapon that was renowned as the "sword that conquered the world." How appropriate then, that this sword became the symbol for the Book that changed the world.

No book has ever made the claims the Bible does; none has enjoyed its distribution or been so widely looked to for inspiration and hope.

> *For the word of God is living and powerful, and sharper than any two-edged sword, piercing even to the division of soul and spirit, and of joints and marrow, and is a discerner of the thoughts and intents of the heart.* Hebrews 4:12

The variety of designs developed for Roman swords demonstrate an important facet of our understanding of God's Word and its use. If we utilize God's Word properly, it will be an awesome weapon and a dependable resource. There certainly are many Bibles available in endless styles, but there is only one inerrant message that God has given to man.

Sharp and Strong

A soldier needed to be sure his sword was sharp and strong; a rusty blade would not do on the battlefield. Likewise, we need to know what the Word of God contains when we pick it up for use. You cannot have confidence in this sword if you doubt the inerrancy of scripture, question the accuracy, and do not trust the infallibility of the Bible. A high view of scripture is mandatory if we are going to put this weapon to proper use.

John MacArthur has this insight about the power of God's Word when it is unleashed:

> "In this imagery, however, it is something more than just a dagger. It is something more than just a small sword. This is a weapon powerful enough to destroy a fortress. And the word there means just that, a massive stone fortress. We assault these fortresses not with human weapons but with weapons that are not even a part of the flesh but rather have as their source and their power divine character. And as a result, we are destroying speculations and every lofty thing raised up against the knowledge of God. What are the fortresses that we attack? They are speculations, *logismos* in the Greek; ideas, theories, viewpoints, any lie, anything that's anti-God, any concept, idea, theory, viewpoint, religion, philosophy that is raised up against the knowledge of God."
> —*Grace To You,* Dr. John MacArthur,
> Message 90-368: "The Armor of God: The Sword of the Spirit"

Just as the Romans had different styles of swords for various combat situations, the Bible uses two terms that are both rendered "word." The one in the Ephesians 6 passage is *rhema*, "a specific word or message from the Bible." *Rhema* connotes a verse that speaks directly to the specific condition or situation of our lives. For example, when you are struggling with a particular situation, perhaps a temptation, God's Word comes to the rescue and speaks directly to you. All of God's revelation in scripture is inspired and inerrant.

All scripture is inspired by God and is profitable for teaching, for reproof, for correction, for training in righteousness. Ephesians 3:16

Another word used in scripture is *logos,* often used to identify "the totality of written scriptures in the Bible, which were given to people under the inspiration of God." This term expresses that the Bible as God's Word is the written, divine expression of revelation about God to humanity as a whole. Jesus fulfilled this expression as the literal incarnation and embodiment of God's Word. When we stand on the Word of God as a whole, trusting its message and meaning, we are using the *logos* as a weapon.

Basic Training

As with other pieces of armor, the sword of the spirit requires faith to be effective. Praying, preaching, and singing the Word are some of the ways it can operate in our lives. Memorization and meditation are two other important techniques of unleashing inspired scriptures.

If we are to take full advantage of what God offers us through His inspired Word, we must be trained and trained well. When the military inducts a new recruit, boot camp is the first stop. Soldiers are not expected to function on the battlefield until they have gone through basic training. Placing proper emphasis on the importance of context in Bible study will help us grasp the full counsel of God's Word. Perhaps the most common mistake that Bible students make is to take a scripture out of context, which leads to an unbalanced view that can become an aberrant view. Balance and context are two tools that must be put into use as we familiarize ourselves with our powerful weapon. Sound study habits should be developed as soon as possible if the soldier is to function at the highest level. Personal study times, regular exposure to trustworthy teaching, and meditating on scripture will all contribute to a solid foundation.

To be a Christian means to be a warrior. Soldiers spend a good amount of time in training and drilling. Ceremonial events and dress uniforms are also part of a soldier's life, but there comes a time when troops must fight; the rest is preparation. The weapons of our spiritual warfare have amazing power, but if their accuracy and potential are not understood, we will not see them used properly.

Into the Battle

It is possible to spend all our time studying, but never applying God's Word. If that's the case, tremendous power will again go to waste. The Bible needs to be both studied and unleashed; that's when we get off the parade field and on to the battlefield.

Since we are fighting a spiritual enemy, this war can only be waged in the invisible realm. Too many saints have struggled for too long addressing the fruit and not the root of their problems. Does that sound like you? Then be encouraged! Help is at hand.

Likewise the Spirit also helps in our weaknesses. For we do not know what we should pray for as we ought, but the Spirit Himself makes intercession for us with groanings which cannot be uttered. Now He who searches the hearts knows what the mind of the Spirit is, because He makes intercession for the saints according to the will of God. Romans 8:26-27

Now that we have learned about the battle, our enemy, and our weapons, we need to understand the nature of the authority we have been granted. Since Satan's judgment was pronounced long ago, and there is not a doubt about his destiny, let's be about the Father's kingdom business.

Every day, the children of this world achieve marvelous progress in technology, science, and business. Corporations don't hesitate to make multi-billion dollar decisions and investments. Skyscrapers are built, gigantic malls are planned, and sprawling subdivisions of homes are designed. It seems like there is no limit to what the world can do when a vision is cast.

How is it then that the church so often has such small dreams? Why do we think we have to convince God to achieve church growth or conduct fruitful outreach? Have you ever noticed that believers are sometimes almost surprised when their prayers are answered? "Wow, someone got saved last night!" Have we missed the concern Jesus displayed for the lost? Do we remember that building the whole church age was heaven's concept in the first place? This is true—we do not have to beg God to display His grace; I believe He is anxious to do so. We know the eyes of the Lord are looking for men and women to be strong on their behalf. Will you be one He finds and uses? Don't be reluctant to pray prayers that our worthy of our God.

Put On the Armor
Shiny armor and a sharp sword are of no value if they remain in a locker. God has told us that in order to defeat Satan, we must put on the whole armor; a belt or a lone breastplate will not work. We need to wear all the armor and be willing to use it. So, how do we actually go about putting these spiritual resources to use? Paul provides this answer:

> *Praying always with all prayer and supplication in the Spirit, being watchful to this end with all perseverance and supplication for all the saints.* Ephesians 6:18

A Divided Enemy
Spiritual resources are appropriated by prayer. Prayer is the comprehensive means by which Christians actualize their spiritual armament. You "get dressed"

95

through prayer. There are many soldiers in God's army who forget their battle gear. A weak prayer life will be reflected in poor performance on the battlefield. As children of God, we certainly can have victory. It has already been granted to us, but God's plan clearly involves the need for us to go out and take hold of the conquest He has engineered. And, one day, the war we are fighting will be over.

> *The work of righteousness will be peace, and the effect of righteousness, quietness and assurance forever.* Isaiah 32:17

In the meantime, there are no college or medical deferments; the battle we face is not for our salvation or our place in heaven—it is a struggle for usefulness, to become all that is intended for us.

Our war is not with a random host of rebellious angels. We face super-powerful sophisticated beings that are highly organized in their hierarchy.

Still, Jesus commented that Satan's house is divided, so we can surmise that it must be difficult for him to coordinate his terrorism. The demonic horde would bring sheer terror to our hearts, but we are to fear no evil. Even though we walk in dangerous territory, the Great Shepherd is with us.

> *Having disarmed principalities and powers, He made a public spectacle of them, triumphing over them in it.* Colossians 2:15

Triumph!

The highest honor a Roman general could be accorded was a Triumph to Rome. The *Dictionary of Roman Antiquities* says: "From the beginning of the Republic to the fall of the Roman Empire, a Triumph was recognized as the summit of military glory, and was the cherished object of every Roman General."

Visitors to Rome today can go to the Via Sacra on the road to the Forum where the landmark Arch of Titus stands. This marbled arch is carved with a scene depicting the triumphal procession awarded to General Titus as he brought the loot from the temple at Jerusalem—the sacred Menorah, the Table of Showbread, and the silver trumpets which called the Jews to Rosh Hashanah. The bearers of the booty wear laurel crowns, and those carrying the candlestick have pillows on their shoulders. Titus was awarded this Triumph for conquering Judea in the Jewish Wars of 66-70 A.D.

A Triumph consisted of a solemn procession when a victorious general came into Rome standing in a chariot drawn by four horses. His troops marched behind him and the vanquished enemy before him. Rome had very specific rules concerning both what military achievement earned this rare honor, and how it was to be conducted.

If a battle met the qualifications, the general would send a laurel-wreathed messenger to the Senate detailing the glories of his conquest. The general would instruct his army to meet him at the gates of Rome, but not enter.

If the Triumph was granted, great care was taken to prepare the day. Banquets, music, and a city-wide celebration surrounded the army's procession to the Senate steps. In the process, the trophy captives, including their leader, would be detoured to a nearby prison and executed while the Roman general went on to a supreme example of exultation and honor. This was the height of glory that Rome could offer.

Some day, Jesus Christ will rule and reign in glory. As soldiers of His, we will be awarded crowns, which we will cast before Him. That will be a day of true and lasting triumph.

Strength and Honor

One of the many advantages that Rome's legions enjoyed was an *esprit de corps*, a sense of larger purpose in defending and enforcing the Roman way. Citizens and soldiers during the Roman ascendancy and supremacy were convinced of the superiority of their civilization. This gave the Roman war machine a cohesion and drive that overwhelmed more loosely organized opponents. Similarly, the church must be convinced that allegiance to truth is worth any sacrifice. Christians are devoted to a cause larger than themselves, and therefore believers earnestly contend for the faith. Romans were often conscripted into their army, but Christian soldiers operate on a volunteer system.

Like a Roman soldier, we not only fight for something, we fight toward something. We stand strong because we want to obey, we battle because we honor heaven, and we wear the armor because we seek to defend God's kingdom on earth.

Beyond these noble motives, we also want to be faithful soldiers because there are eternal rewards for doing so. We too are offered a "triumph" on a scale far beyond any earthly event. The apostle John hoped that his spiritual children would enjoy an "abundant entry" into heaven.

General Titus never enjoyed the monument erected in his honor; his arch was constructed posthumously, while the Christian soldier will certainly have all eternity to savor the rewards of service to the King.

14

The Ultimate Ally

Groanings which cannot be uttered are often prayers which cannot be refused.
—*C.H. Spurgeon*

As we draw close to the end of our study of spiritual warfare, it is wise to pause again on the topic of prayer. There is no more worthy exercise of spiritual power than answering the call to prayer.

The book of Ephesians opens with a wonderful invitation to life in the heights of God's high places:

Blessed be the God and Father of our Lord Jesus Christ, who has blessed us with every spiritual blessing in the heavenly places in Christ. Ephesians 1:3

From this lofty position, we are taken to the close of Ephesians where we end on our knees.

Though there are numerous passages in the Bible that elaborate on the wonderful promises associated with prayer, we really need only to obey a simple command of Jesus:

Watch and pray always... Luke 21:36

The Nuclear Option

It was August 9, 1945 when an atomic bomb was last used offensively on planet earth. Since that day, a number of nations have tested weapons and joined the nuclear club, and the power of these bombs has grown significantly. Yet, thankfully, restraint has kept these destructive weapons from being used.

The principle here is fitting, because the church has been given an amazingly powerful weapon in the form of prayer. It is a privilege and an opportunity without limits, when it is used properly. There is a long list of scriptures that attest to the remarkable invitation to pray. Prayer is also a power that terrifies our enemy. And here is where the illustration of atomic power does apply: sometimes Christians use this weapon infrequently and keep it on the shelf.

Confess your trespasses to one another, and pray for one another, that you may be healed. The effective, fervent prayer of a righteous man avails much. James 5:16

Clear and to the point, prayer works, so use it! We need every kind of prayer and we need to be willing to pray at all times. Publicly and privately, out loud and in your heart, pray always. We can thank, praise, ask, confess and adore. Prayer can happen in all kinds of positions, kneeling, walking or sitting, with eyes closed or open.

Whatever our situation may be, we need to pray. The length of prayer is not the issue.

Peter prayed one of the shortest yet most effective prayers ever, "Lord, save me!," when he was sinking on the lake.

There was no doubt about what Peter needed at that moment. He knew what to pray without question. We do not always have that clarity. There are issues so complicated in our lives that we do not know what to pray. That is when the Holy Spirit comes to our rescue. The Spirit knows how to pray and what to pray for. We do not know how to pray as we should, but again, Romans 8:26 tells us that the Spirit Himself intercedes for us with groanings too deep for words. What a great comfort and relief that we can release our prayers to the Spirit and trust that they will be guided and directed for our best.

Praying in the Spirit means praying in harmony and perfect accord with the mind of the Spirit of God and the will of God. This is personal assistance from the Trinity that assures us that even when we do not know the will of God, we can effectively pray with the help of the Holy Spirit.

This assistance is not always needed because we do know the revealed will of God on many subjects. We know we are called to be pure, to be strong and to be in service to others. Praying that we will have strength to overcome temptation is very clear and this power is available to us. However, when we need guidance to pray about a decision we are unsure of, the Holy Spirit is there to help.

Bold Prayer

Prayer, by nature, is an act of faith, and it is also a bold venture, well-illustrated in a parable told by Jesus:

And He said to them, "Which of you shall have a friend, and go to him at midnight and say to him, 'Friend, lend me three loaves; for a friend of mine has come to me on his journey, and I have nothing to set before him'; and he will answer from within and say, 'Do not trouble me; the door is now shut, and my children are with me in bed; I cannot rise and give to you'? I say to you, though he will not rise and give to him because he is his friend, yet because of his persistence he will rise and give him as many as he needs.

"So I say to you, ask, and it will be given to you; seek, and you will find; knock, and it will be opened to you. For everyone who asks receives, and he who seeks finds, and to him who knocks it will be opened. If a son asks for bread from any father among you, will he give him a stone? Or if he asks for a fish, will he give him a serpent instead of a fish? Or if he asks for an egg, will he offer him a scorpion? If you then, being evil, know how to give good gifts to your children, how much more will your heavenly Father give the Holy Spirit to those who ask Him!"
Luke 11:5-15

Bold and Brief

When Jesus told this story, He had just concluded a teaching about how to pray, which raised the question of attitude in prayer. How should we feel about prayer? Should we grovel? So, while He was perhaps in the same location, and certainly on the same subject, Jesus launched right into a parable with an easy-to-understand message.

Let's set the stage. In ancient Israel, it was common to be dependent on your neighbors. There were no twenty-four hour grocery stores. If you had a need, it was customary to call upon someone nearby. Since the economy was often day-to-day, families made enough bread for the day and people often existed by hand-to-mouth survival.

That was the situation here—a neighbor ran out of food, and it was not a good time for a visit next door. Remember, there was no electricity in this time, so when the sun when down, bedtime was not far behind. You basically stayed up a short while with some light from a candle, and then you went to sleep, because work began early. The fact is, nobody was awake at midnight.

It might be easier for us to relate to this story if we imagine a late-night phone call with a request to give a friend help. Perhaps they are out of gas or broken down in their car. Not a welcome interruption, but one that cannot be ignored.

"Lend me three loaves" (v. 5). The needy neighbor wants three pieces of flat bread, which would be sufficient for an evening meal. Clearly, this is not an emergency. No one is starving to death; this is a wild request. Would you go next door for a midnight snack? There is more to the story than that, however, because he goes on to say, "For a friend of mine has come to me from a journey and I have nothing to set before him."

Due to the extreme daytime heat in that area of the world, it was not unusual for travel to take place at night. So, this journey ended at midnight, setting off a chain of events that are very instructive for us today.

Hospitality was expected in the ancient world, and even more so within Jewish society. Care for a stranger was an important part of their law and customs.

Protocol is one thing, but obedience is another, especially at midnight. This is important background for the proper understanding of what took place next.

Knock, Seek, Ask

Now the action shifts to the other side of the door in this mini-drama, "And from inside he shall answer..." (v. 7). So this conversation is going on through the door, and the friend is saying, "Do not bother me. The door has already been shut and my children and I are in bed. I cannot get up and give you anything." Well, this is hard for the neighbor, because he might end up being a poor host.

The door has already been shut. Here we need to imagine a door that is more complicated than our contemporary variety. This door was probably a drop-down model that was quite noisy when it was shut. And so the reply comes, "My children and I are in bed."

The entire episode seems very aggressive and quite troubling. It's not a true emergency, and is it that crucial for the visitor to have food at midnight? It really does not seem unreasonable for the man to say, "I'm not going to get up and give you anything. This is too much trouble."

Jesus then takes us to the heart of the matter by observing, "I tell you, even though he will not get up and give him anything because he is his friend, yet because of his persistence [importunity or boldness] he will get up and give him as much as he needs" (v. 8).

Midnight Boldness

Wow, what brashness and nerve! The emphasis here is on his boldness—and this is the core of the lesson. It's the boldness of asking at such an inconvenient time, and we can see that it certainly took a lot of courage to intrude at this hour.

The illustration is of shameless, bold, importunity— these attitudes relate to us going into the presence of God. Jesus is teaching us how to have the freedom of ceaseless prayer. When we hear the admonition to pray without ceasing, very often the emphasis is on how we can accomplish this. But, what about the other side of the prayer equation? Are we free to pray to God 24/7? Yes! We have to ask, but He wants to listen!

In our story, this man responded, not because of friendship, but because of annoyance. Unlike the irritated neighbor, we never wake God up. He is always available, and more than that, always willing to hear from His children.

Now Jesus unloads the punch line, "And I say to you, ask and it shall be given you, seek and you shall find, knock and it shall be opened to you, for everyone who asks receives and he who seeks finds, and to him who knocks it shall be opened" (v. 9-10). This is truly a surprise—it's not a rebuke. We should be forever thankful that heaven does not operate on a nine-to-five basis, doesn't take off for holidays, and will never turn a sincere seeker away. Knock, seek, and ask; this simple three-point outline can supercharge our prayer life.

Are you willing to be bold and knock loudly for your need? Will you relentlessly seek God's will when you need direction? Then ask with firm faith when you are praying to follow the revealed will of the Lord.

This short story is overflowing with applications that are easy to follow, especially if we operate in the knowledge that we have the favor of God. So ask, please ask; Heaven is anxious to answer the prayer of faith.

The Ultimate Ally

Living here in Colorado Springs, I am always reminded of the natural beauty God has blessed this region with. Pikes Peak towers over our city as the Rocky Mountains provide a gorgeous backdrop to the west. This city also is full of reminders of the presence of the United States military. NORAD, Fort Carson, and the Air Force Academy are just three of the major installations nearby. We don't know about all the systems and weapons that operate here, but what we do know is very impressive.

The Eye in the Sky

America's space technology includes the ability to look into every nation with great accuracy from the sky. This satellite system in synchronous orbit around earth gives our nation an incredible advantage in any conflict. Any military strategist will tell you that, historically, the army that has the high ground is generally the victor. The ability to observe the enemy and prepare for their movements provides an almost unbeatable edge.

Now, let's make the obvious application to the spiritual. King David knew there was no way to escape the presence of God; He is everywhere. Despite the fact that our ancient parents forfeited the glorious authority that was granted to them in the garden, the church benefits from being on the right side of biblical history. The legally-lost kingdom authority has been rightfully restored, and we have an ally that cannot be overcome. God sees every device of Satan, every weakness of our flesh, and every path we can take to victory.

We need only to have the simple wisdom to learn of Him, and to call upon Him, then to see Him be strong in our behalf.

Submission Is the Key

No army can operate for long without observation of the chain of command. Anyone familiar with military order knows that rank and authority are strictly observed. Submission to military authority is not optional; it is crucial to the operation of any army.

That's where our total submission to God comes in. If we are going to benefit from the advantages offered by God's exclusive attributes, such as "eye in the sky" omniscience, we must submit to His total ownership and authority. Unquestioned obedience is the stock and trade of any soldier, and in our case, more than grudging submission is required. God wants His children to so completely trust Him that they cheerfully submit.

Learning to yield to God and His Holy Spirit is a lifelong pursuit, one that only comes from experience and knowledge. These two go hand-in-hand; neither can stand alone. We must learn all we can about what God has said about Himself in scripture. This knowledge will provide a reservoir of faith. Then we must act on these truths and experience how living faith works in the real world.

Faith without works is dead. James 2:20 (b)

Onward Christian Soldiers

The Church Age is currently in a time of militancy. We are at war, as we have learned in the course of this study. Someday, we will see the transformation to the Church Triumphant, but for now we must march and learn to function as a living unit, the Body of Christ. This is the most marvelous organization on earth, with Jesus Christ as the head—or General, for the sake of our illustration.

So, as we bring this journey in for a landing, let's review these important bullet points:

• Fear of our enemy can be replaced by confidence.

- Satan seeks to prevent you from fulfilling your spiritual potential.

- Victory is possible over habits, anxiety, and condemnation.

- We have the power to exercise authority over our will, mind, and natural emotions.

- We have what we need to win the battles we face.

Everything we encounter in this life as a Christian is in preparation for the climactic, glorious revelation of Jesus Christ as King.

Eventually and inevitably, Jesus will be enthroned, Satan will be finally and fully cast out, and the world will be as God intended from the very beginning.

15

Dress for Success

"Jesus Christ has set me free from the chains of sin." —LAILAH GIFTY AKITA

Let us imagine you have been invited to a significant social event, a real black-tie gala.

Or perhaps it is your first day at work at a new job that is a real promotion.

What is one of the first things you might think about on such occasions?

"What will I wear?" And this concern is not just true of the ladies!

As a Christian, you have accepted an invitation to a huge, major event. The Bible speaks to us in our language. When Jesus told the story of the wedding banquet in Matthew 22:11-13, the problem with the gate-crasher was his attire.

"Friend, how did you come in here without wedding clothes?"

This guy was evicted from the premises. Anyone planning to attend the "wedding feast of the Lamb" should pay heed to the moral of this story, which is hinted at in the following passage.

Let us be glad and rejoice and give Him glory, for the marriage of the Lamb has come, and His wife has made herself ready." And to her it was granted to be arrayed in fine linen, clean and bright, for the fine linen is the righteous acts of the saints. Revelation 17:7-9

The Bible has a good bit to say about clothing.

High priests were elegantly and intricately clothed.

Jesus warned about religious leaders who sought the outward appearance of long robes; no one gets past the angel bouncers in heaven without robes of righteousness, cleansed in the blood of the Lamb.

"Take away the filthy garments from him." And to him he said, "See, I have removed your iniquity from you, and I will clothe you with rich robes." Zechariah 3:4 (b)

And then there is the prodigal son, who was immediately given regal robes by his dad upon repentance.

A lot of folks spend a great deal of time, effort and expense on their wardrobes, hair, and cosmetics.

All that glory will surely fade-and fast! You need to

make prepare for appearing before God Himself.

Paul wrote in 2 Corinthians 5:9 that we "must" all appear before the judgment seat of Christ, and you need to be ready for that.

What Kind of Crown?

Once you have been assured entrance to heaven by way of accepting the forgiveness offered by Jesus Christ, the "dress code" question is resolved, you have been issued your robe. Rejoice!

But wait there is more to this plan.

The purpose of preparing and engaging in the spiritual warfare we have been discussing is not simply an exercise to bide our time on earth.

God does not create busy work for His people.

This is not a dress rehearsal, life is preparation for eternity, and how we conduct ourselves here will, in some marvelous and mysterious way impact how we experience the next life.

The Bible promises another article of clothing to those who are faithful in this life: crowns.

Five specific crowns are described in scripture as being available to believers in Jesus.

Crown of Righteousness

I have fought the good fight, I have finished the race, I have kept the faith. Finally, there is laid up for me the crown of righteousness, which the Lord, the righteous Judge, will give to me on that Day, and not to me only but also to all who have loved His appearing. 2 Timothy 4:7-8

This crown will be given to those who lived a life that glorified God while on earth.

No one is perfect for now, but there are Christians who are in right standing with God, yet are not living righteous lives on a daily basis here on earth. These people chronically and consistently make choices that are in conflict with clearly revealed principles of scripture. This is not an occasional stumble or unusual aberrant behavior; this carnal, conflicting lifestyle wants sure admittance to heaven while putting selfish pleasures on earth as a priority.

On the other hand, there are those who earnestly seek to please God with their time on earth, not for the purpose of earning salvation, but to glorify their Savior. These are the people who will be seen wearing crowns of righteousness in heaven.

The Incorruptible Crown

Do you not know that those who run in a race all run, but one receives the prize? Run in such a way that you may obtain it. And everyone who competes for the prize is temperate in all things.

Now they do it to obtain a perishable crown, but we for an imperishable crown. Therefore I run thus: not with uncertainty. Thus I fight: not as one who beats the air. But I discipline my body and bring it into subjection, lest, when I have preached to others, I myself should become disqualified. 1 Corinthians 9:24-27

This may also be called the "victor's crown."

Athletes understand that preparation, commitment and sacrifice are required to compete effectively.

The Apostle Paul often equated the Christian life with an athletic event that has a rewards ceremony to honor and greet the victor.

This crown is granted to those who are willing to sacrifice for the sake of completing the mission that God has called them to do.

The Crown of Life

Do not fear any of those things which you are about to suffer. Indeed, the devil is about to throw some of you into prison, that you may be tested, and you will have tribulation ten days. Be faithful until death, and I will give you the crown of life. Revelation 2:10

This crown has been known as the "martyr's crown."

Jesus said He will give this reward to those who go through severe testing, torture and even death because of their testimony.

The Crown of Rejoicing

For what is our hope, or joy, or CROWN OF REJOICING? Is it not even you in the presence of our Lord Jesus Christ at His coming? For you are our glory and joy. 1 Thessalonians 2:19-20

This may be called the "soul winners crown."

In the classic science fiction program, "Star Trek," there was a "prime directive," to boldly explore new worlds without interfering with the civilizations.

Everything Captain Kirk and the crew did was filtered through this command.

Christians have the Great Commission and this should be our overriding principle.

However, our directive is the absolute opposite of the adventures of the Enterprise, we want to interfere to the absolute maximum with all of mankind. We want to change their eternal direction.

To those who make evangelism their life goal, they will be granted this crown.

Crown of Glory

The elders who are among you I exhort, I who am a fellow elder and a witness of the sufferings of Christ, and also a partaker of the glory that will be revealed. Shepherd the flock which is among you, serving as overseers, not by constraint but willingly, not for dishonest gain but eagerly; nor as being lords over those entrusted to you, but being examples to the flock; and when the Chief Shepherd appears, you will receive the crown of glory that does not fade away. 1 Peter 5:1-4

This crown is offered to the elders, teachers and shepherds among the church. From the pulpit to the nursery, from the mission field to the coffee-shop Bible study, there are men and women who may or may not be on full-time church staff. But they aren't concerned about a paycheck here; they are serving for the reward of their Chief Shepherd in that great day to come.

This is the crown of glory.

Finally, Stand

In the 1980's, the book, *Dress for Success,* was a runaway bestseller. Salespeople, executives and businesses far and wide poured over the pages to get an advantage in their world.

Christians are looking for a different kingdom, reward and crown.

The spiritual armor we have described is provided so that we might have spiritual stability.

Three times in our key verse from Ephesians, the Bible says: "Stand." For example:

Therefore take up the whole armor of God, that you may be able to withstand in the evil day, and having done all, to stand. Ephesians 6:13

It is my hope and prayer that as you continue with the Lord, you will start by standing, strapping on the armor and walking worthy of the great calling upon your life.

That is the way to dress for eternal success.